Documents and Debates
National Socialism in Germany

D0293575

SWANSEA COLLEGE

Documents and Debates

The original titles in the series (still available)

For the extended series, see the back cover of this book.

Documents and Debates
General Editor: John Wroughton M.A., F.R.Hist.S.

National Socialism in Germany

Niall Rothnie

Head of History, King Edward VI School, Bath

MACMILLAN

First published 1987
Reprinted 1988, 1990, 1991

Published by
MACMILLAN EDUCATION LTD
Houndmills, Basingstoke, Hampshire RG21 2XS
and London
Companies and representatives
throughout the world

Printed in Hong Kong

British Library Cataloguing in Publication Data
Rothnie, Niall
National socialism in Germany.—
(Documents and debates)
1. National socialism—History
2. Germany—Politics and government—
1918-1933   3. Germany—Politics and
government—1933-1945
I. Title   II. Series
335.6'0943   DD240
ISBN 0–333–41248–6

Contents

General Editor's Preface

This book forms part of a series entitled *Documents and Debates*, which is aimed primarily at sixth formers. The earlier volumes in the series each covered approximately one century of history, using material both from original documents and from modern historians. The more recent volumes, however, are designed in response to the changing trends in history examinations at 18 plus, most of which now demand the study of documentary sources and the testing of historical skills. Each volume therefore concentrates on a particular topic within a narrow span of time. It consists of eight sections, each dealing with a major theme in depth, illustrated by extracts drawn from primary sources. The series intends partly to provide experience from those pupils who are required to answer questions on documentary material at A-level, and partly to provide pupils of all abilities with a digestible and interesting collection of source material, which will extend the normal textbook approach.

This book is designed essentially for the pupil's own personal use. The author's introduction will put the period as a whole into perspective, highlighting the central issues, main controversies, available source material and recent developments. Although it is clearly not our intention to replace the traditional textbook, each section will carry its own brief introduction, which will set the documents into context. A wide variety of source material has been used in order to give the pupils the maximum amount of experience – letters, speeches, newspapers, memoirs, diaries, official papers, Acts of Parliament, Minute Books, accounts, local documents, family papers, etc. The questions vary in difficulty, but aim throughout to compel the pupil to think in depth by the use of unfamiliar material. Historical knowledge and understanding will be tested, as well as basic comprehension. Pupils will also be encouraged by the questions to assess the reliability of evidence, to recognise bias and emotional prejudice, to reconcile conflicting accounts and to extract the essential from the irrelevant. Some questions, *marked with an asterisk*, require knowledge outside the immediate extract and are intended for further research or discussion, based on the pupil's general knowledge of the period. Finally, we hope that students using this material will learn something of the nature of historical inquiry and the role of the historian.

John Wroughton

Acknowledgements

The author and publishers wish to thank the following who have kindly given permission for the use of copyright material; George Allen & Unwin Ltd. for an extract from *Nazis and Germans* by H. Picton, 1940; Associated Book Publishers (UK) Ltd. for extracts from *Hitler Speaks* by H. Rausching, Thornton Butterworth, 1939; *A History of National Socialism* by K. Heiden, Eyre and Spottiswoode, 1934; and *Thus Spake Germany* by W. Coole and M. Potter, Routledge and Kegan Paul, 1941; Jonathan Cape Ltd. for extracts from *Hitler and I* by Otto Strasser, trans. by Gwenda David, 1940; Century Hutchinson Ltd. for extracts from *The Political Testament of Hermann Goering* trans. by H. W. Blood-Ryan, John Long Ltd., 1938; from *Reaching for the Stars* by N. Waln, The Cresset Press Ltd., 1940; from *Germany's Hitler* by Heinz A. Heinz, Hurst and Blackett, 1934; and from *Mein Kampf* by Adolf Hitler, Hurst and Blackett, 1939; André Deutsch Ltd. for an extract from *Memoirs* by F. von Papen, 1952; Europa Verlag Zurich for extracts from *Adolf Hitler* Vols. 1 and 2 by Konrad Heiden; William Heinemann Ltd. for extracts from *Hitler's Letters and Notes* by W. Maser, 1974; Macmillan Publishing Co. Inc. for extracts from *Years of Reckoning* by G. Ward Price originally published by Cassell & Co. Ltd., 1939; Oxford University Press for extracts from *Speeches on Foreign Policy* by Viscount Halifax, ed. H. H. E. Craster, 1940; Laurence Pollinger Ltd. on behalf of Karl Ludecke for extracts from *I Knew Hitler*, Jarrolds Publishers Ltd., 1938; The Royal Institute of International Affairs for extracts from *The Speeches of Adolf Hitler* Vols. 1 and 2, trans. and ed. N. Baynes, Oxford University Press for RIIA, 1942; Raymond Savage Ltd. on behalf of the late Sir Neville Henderson for extracts from *Failure of a Mission*, Hodder and Stoughton, 1940; Tessa Sayle on behalf of the estate of G. Ward Price for extracts from *I Knew These Dictators*, Harrap Ltd., 1937; University of Exeter for extracts from *Nazism 1919–1945* Vols. 1 and 2 eds. J. Noakes and G. Pridham; The University of North Carolina Press for a table from *The Nazi Voter: The Social Foundations of Fascism in Germany 1919–1933* by T. Childers, Copyright 1983 The University of North Carolina Press; Weidenfeld (Publishers) Ltd. for extracts from *Inside the*

Third Reich by Albert Speer, 1970; from *Hitler* by J. Fest, 1974: and from *The Nazi Persecution of the Churches* by J. Conway, 1968.

National Socialism in Germany

The Thousand Year Reich lasted in reality barely thirteen years; yet there are few historical subjects which engender so much interest still. A person with no interest whatsoever in history will still have heard not only of Adolf Hitler but also of leading associates such as Joseph Goebbels and Heinrich Himmler and terms such as S.S., Brown Shirts, concentration camps and the Swastika. The Nazis remain a topic of, at times perhaps, unhealthy interest, and yet when one tries to look beyond the known, surface details, one seems to enter a labyrinth of confusion and argument, as historians present new interpretations, often in direct contradiction to previous ones.

One problem is that there is a wealth of documentation on the Nazis in Germany. This might appear to be an advantage – at least we know what happened. Yet it is always dangerous to take a document at face value. A continuing theme in this volume of documents is that one must not only ask what is being said, but why: what reasons has the author for writing this document? The private, honest thoughts of a key participant in an event, written without the benefit of hindsight are the dream of every historian: unfortunately genuine Hitler diaries have yet to turn up. All source material is biased; and historians will still disagree over what degree of bias is involved; and what the writer actually meant by what he said.

You are probably, hopefully, approaching this book with a working knowledge of Nazi Germany. You may know of the major events; yet there will still be arguments over motive and explanation. Did the Nazis burn down the Reichstag? How far were they involved in the killing of Dollfuss? Was there an S.A. plot to take over the state forestalled by the Night of the Long Knives? General controversies have generated even more heat.

This book uses a wide selection of available evidence with, often, open-ended questions, and yet it is a selection in itself. Hitler's *Mein Kampf* is an obvious source being his only major piece of writing and easily accessible. Hence, perhaps, its overuse by anthologists when Hitler deliberately wrote it for publication and later admitted that much of it no longer represented his views. His speeches tend to be direct appeals to whatever the audience happened to be at the time. Hitler was very good at attempting to be all things to all people and it would be a brave historian who would claim to find one speech or letter that summed up all of Hitler's views. This idea of key documents by or about Hitler is perfectly represented by the Hossbach memorandum. Is it a blueprint for aggression or a pep talk for reluctant government leaders? It is worth remembering that it was quoted at the Nuremburg trials, where many volumes of selected documents were produced to prove Nazi guilt. With stories of documents embarrassing to the allied cause being secretly destroyed before the trials, it must be remembered that much of the documentation from the German archives freely available today has been circulated to prove one point or another against the Nazis.

There are speeches, letters and, in Goebbels' case for example, diaries from many of the Nazi leaders. But apart from the aforementioned problems with any type of document it was also in Hitler's nature to encourage diversification and, in extreme cases, disputes amongst his followers. A policy of divide and rule may have helped Hitler but it is hard for the historian to judge which, if any, of Hitler's chief ministers was speaking official policy.

What of outsiders? There are those who knew them and then went their own way – Otto Strasser, Fritz Thyssen – but too often they had their own axe to grind and some such as Heiden and Rauschning have had severe doubts cast on their veracity. Those who did not know Hitler can produce dispassionate accounts, but without real knowledge of why the Führer did a particular act. Many believed the propaganda and if a fair number of the authors quoted here appear to take a favourable view towards Hitler then one must remember that during this period mass warfare and mass extermination had not yet begun. Without the benefit of hindsight, even Hitler's critics here accuse him mostly of bullying rather than organised murders. With hindsight, those Nazi supporters that did survive the war have tended to heap all the blame on Hitler and none on themselves. A number of postwar accounts are included here to remind us that we should not always believe what we read.

One of the most interesting points when one reads the more critical extracts is the fact that outsiders such as the British ambassador, Horace Rumbold, and the American, William Dodd, were already raising many of the questions that continue to plague historians today. There are many arguments but perhaps they can be summarised in terms of two views of human nature, the optimistic and the pessimistic. The optimistic view sees Hitler and the Nazis as an aberration in history. Hitler, a twisted genius, began with a few like-minded followers, who laid the blame for their personal shortcomings and the outcome of World War I on the convenient scapegoat of the Weimar Republic. A fringe party, they stood little chance of success until the Wall Street Crash occurred and people turned in desperation to this unknown but untried party, the Nazis. Even then they gained no majority vote but Hitler came to power by the stupidity and duplicity of leading politicians, chancellor von Papen in particular, who saved the Nazis just when they were beginning to lose support. Violence then brought Hitler total power and intimidation kept the majority of the people cowed while clever propaganda kept them confused and under control. Meanwhile Hitler concentrated on foreign policy, his megalomania and desire to take over the world finally meeting resistance from Britain and France with the start of World War II. Thus the majority of the German people never directly, or willingly, supported the Nazis who imposed themselves on the people.

What might be seen as a more depressing view of human nature stresses less the idea of aberration, more the frightening normality of the Nazis and their general acceptance by the German people. This view stresses the lack of longterm Nazi plans, the idea that Hitler made up his policies as he went along and that the death camps were never a predetermined horror. This idea works from the same initial premise of a fringe party but stresses Hitler's basic intelligence and cunning. Learning from the fiasco of the Munich Putsch, he skilfully rebuilt the party to create an effective framework for further expansion. He reacted to events to gain power. The Wall Street Crash was important but the public knew he advocated the use of violence and made a conscious decision to vote for him. He never gained a majority but then few winning parties in Western democracy ever do so. He did lead the largest party and it was natural to offer him the post of chancellor. Total power was accepted by many of the public who felt desperate situations required desperate remedies. The economy boomed and the people, prosperous and employed, were happy. This must have been so, for the argument runs that Hitler's government was relatively weak and needed popular support. Anti-semitism was played down by Hitler once in power as it was a vote-loser. His foreign policy was unplanned, helped by allied mistakes, based on a natural desire to change the Treaty of Versailles or the traditional policy of Lebensraum in east Europe. Hitler was merely more successful than previous German leaders. By this view the Nazis did not come to power because the public did not understand their views; but because they did.

Few would choose to paint such a black and white picture; most would agree with some 'pessimistic' views but also find some truth in the more 'optimistic' features. This collection hopes to give some food for thought and to lead the reader through the main themes of Hitler and Nazi Germany. Accordingly, the first chapter deals with the Nazis' early years culminating in the blind alley of the Munich Putsch. The next chapter looks at the rebuilding of the party and how it took advantage of the Wall Street Crash to achieve electoral success. The internal machinations leading to Hitler becoming chancellor come next followed by the moves that brought him total power. Domestic policy is divided into those measures that brought Hitler popularity, especially the economy, and then those ways in which any opposition could be stifled. Foreign policy, again, is in two chapters and considers Hitler's motives and then contrasts them with his actual policies.

Any division such as this can impose an order where there actually was none, or a different order to that which really existed. To divide foreign policy at 1937, for example, might reinforce the old idea of a peaceful foreign policy up to that year and a more bellicose one thereafter. But if you are ready to argue against this division then you should be prepared to support your arguments, however tentative they may be. Most questions here are open-ended; to some extent so are many of the themes. There is room for many views based on many forms of evidence as well as the interpretation of this evidence. Of course, you cannot just put forward a theory without supporting evidence, but do consider one thing first; was Hitler a one-off, an accident in history; or is there the potential for being a Nazi in all of us?

I   The Early Years, 1918–24

Introduction

From its foundation after World War I, the Weimar Republic never lacked enemies. Indeed, some historians have marvelled that it lasted as long as it did, seeing it as an illogical development in Germany after centuries of authoritarian rule. The new republic lacked a broad base of support. The left wing felt that it was not radical enough; the right wing felt that Weimar was too radical and that it had betrayed the country by agreeing to the Versailles peace treaty.

It is a standard question to ask whether Weimar was doomed from the start. Yet in the first five years or so, if largely backed by American loans, it did do well and under the skilled leadership of Gustav Stresemann even the Ruhr occupation was terminated, albeit on the resumption of reparation payments.

During this period, therefore, the Nazi party was merely one of many agitating against the government and not a very important one at that. Anton Drexler's German Workers' Party appears to have been no more than a group of drinking companions with an antipathy to many modern 'isms', communism and liberalism in particular. Hitler's main contribution was to organise this group far more efficiently and to turn it into a proper party with at least pretensions to power. His beliefs are more difficult to summarise especially when much of his programme was merely an attack on present institutions and attitudes and, if some contemporaries are to be believed, his positive demands were anything that would get him support: the socialist aspect of Nazism has always remained vague. Even major aspects such as racism could be toned down when the situation demanded. Hitler himself disliked being tied down to specific policies and one can attach too much weight to programmes such as the 25 Points.

Hitler's oratory, organisational skills and refusal to share power led to the absorption of a number of similarly minded small parties in the next few years. With the S.A. and the support of the war hero General Ludendorf, Hitler decided to take advantage of the government's capitulation over the Ruhr occupation to march on Berlin. The Nazis never got further than the Odeonplatz in

Munich. With the benefit of hindsight, Hitler may have learnt a lot from this failure; but the debacle pushed the Nazis back into the political wilderness for the next few years.

1 The shortcomings of Weimar

(a) Hitler on the German Revolution

The main body of the Social Democratic horde occupied the conquered positions, and the Independent Socialist and Spartacist storm battalions were side-tracked.

But that did not happen without a struggle.

5 The activist assault formations that had started the Revolution were dissatisfied and felt that they had been betrayed. They now wanted to continue the fight on their own account. But their illimitable racketeering became odious even to the wire-pullers of the Revolution. For the Revolution itself had scarcely been
10 accomplished when two camps appeared. In the one camp were the elements of peace and order; in the other were those of blood and terror. Was it not perfectly natural that our bourgeoisie should rush with flying colours to the camp of peace and order? For once in their lives their piteous political organizations found it possible
15 to act, inasmuch as the ground had been prepared for them on which they were glad to get a new footing; and thus to a certain extent they found themselves in coalition with that power which they hated but feared. The German political bourgeoisie achieved the high honour of being able to associate itself with the accursed
20 Marxist leaders for the purpose of combating Bolshevism.

Thus the following state of affairs took shape as early as December 1918 and January 1919:

A minority constituted of the worst elements had made the Revolution. And behind this minority all the Marxist parties
25 immediately fell into step. The Revolution itself had an outward appearance of moderation, which aroused against it the enmity of the fanatical extremists. These began to launch hand-grenades and fire machine-guns, occupying public buildings, and thus threatening to destroy the moderate appearance of the Revolution. To prevent
30 this terror from developing further a truce was concluded between the representatives of the new regime and the adherents of the old order, so as to be able to wage a common fight against the extremists. The result was that the enemies of the Republic ceased to oppose the Republic as such and helped to subjugate those who
35 were also enemies of the Republic, though for quite different reasons. But a further result was that all danger of the adherents of the old State putting up a fight against the new was now definitely averted.

This fact must always be clearly kept in mind. Only by
40 remembering it can we understand how it was possible that a
nation in which nine-tenths of the people had not joined in a
revolution, where seven-tenths repudiated it and six-tenths detested
it – how this nation allowed the Revolution to be imposed upon it
by the remaining one-tenth of the population.

  Adolf Hitler, *Mein Kampf* (London, Hurst and Blackett,
  1939), p 434

(b) Heiden on the German Revolution

45 Nowhere, with the exception of Russia, did the State destroy
property as radically as in Germany. And it was not the workers
who did it. Not the Social Democrats, who in 1918 had proclaimed
the republic; or the Communists, who reviled the Social Democrats
as 'traitors to the working class', and for years kept disturbing the
50 peace with vain, hopeless attempts at revolt. The workers had no
intention at all of destroying property. Plans to this effect stood in
the party programmes, but nowhere else. For the proletarian is a
component of the capitalist economy, and what he wishes is not
to abolish exploiting capitalism, but to exploit it himself.
55 On November 9, 1918, Philipp Scheidemann, the Social
Democratic leader, proclaimed the republic in Berlin saying, 'The
German people has been victorious all along the line'; but a week
later the leaders of the German working class, who had been
victorious all along the line, concluded a pact with the leaders of
60 the German employers 'for the maintenance of our economic life'.
And both sides solemnly declared 'that the reconstruction of our
national economy requires the pooling of all economic and
intellectual forces and the harmonious collaboration of all'. It
could not have been said more clearly: to save capitalism from the
65 crushing vice of war socialism was the aim of the workers as well
as the capitalists.
  At this time Socialist demonstrations were swarming through
the capital; as the masses passed through the Tiergarten, the great
park in the middle of Berlin, a voice is said to have cried out:
70 'Comrades, preserve revolutionary discipline! Don't walk on the
grass!' A legend perhaps. But how apt!

  K. Heiden, *Hitler, A Biography* (New York, Alfred A.
  Knopf, 1936), p 108

Questions

a Why, according to Hitler in extract *a*, did the middle classes
  join with and support the 'Marxist leaders' (line 20)?
b Which 'adherents of the old order' (lines 31–2) did support the
  new socialist government and why?

★ c Were the events of late 1918 a 'Revolution' as Hitler claims?
   d How does extract *b* take a different view of the same events described in extract *a*?
   e What is the purpose of the story told in lines 67–71?
★ f Basing your answer on these extracts and other sources known to you do you think Weimar's problem was that it was too radical or that it was not radical enough?

2   The German Workers' Party

An interview with Anton Drexler

'Perhaps I ought to say that our Party didn't really aspire – yet – to be a party. It only consisted of the committee of six men. But, of course, we couldn't make any sort of headway. Our meetings were private because of this Red threat. We seemed to have got
5 ourselves into a blind alley. We could do little but discuss and study. I embodied my own ideas in a slight brochure called *Mein politisches Erwachen. From the diary of a working man.'*

Here Drexler turns to a drawer in his writing desk and brings a copy of it into the light. A little affair, this, of some forty pages
10 bound in a tattered blue cover.

'Let me read you a bit' says the author eagerly, 'just one or two of the most telling passages –'

'Oh, no, first I ought to make it clear that this didn't pretend to lay down lines for a Party exactly. I only aimed really at setting
15 down the views and thoughts of a starred man of the street, of the War, the Front, and the Revolution, and to draw out the necessary consequences –'

Then he reads, jumping from page to page (the book is evidently known to him by heart), and I gather the impression of
20 a hefty invective against usury, profiteering, cowardice, and class privilege. . . . The whole thing, I know, merely voiced the passionate conviction of hundreds and thousands of inarticulate workers here at home in Germany. It suggested, however, no solution for the problems so trenchantly envisaged and presented.
25 How could a group consisting of merely six men, with no following worth speaking of, and no representation in the Landtag, make its voice heard in the political world at that time?

No one was more aware of the futility of it all than Anton Drexler in 1919.
30 'If only someone would turn up,' he breaks off reading and resumes his story, 'I used to think if only someone would turn up with go and grit in him, we could make something out of us and this,' slapping the pamphlet, 'and contrive a real driving force behind us. It would need to be an outstanding personality,
35 anyhow, who could even attempt to do such a thing, a man of

intense conviction, single-eyed, and absolutely fearless. I never
really hoped or dreamed that such an individual would ever blow
in at the Sterneckerbräu! A genius such as we needed – such as
Germany needed – only turns up once in a century!'
40   'My goodness, but it is well known now – that story . . . of
our little meeting at eight o'clock one evening in the Sterneckerbräu,
when Feder got up to speak! First there'd been a bit of a clash
between our first speaker – who suggested a union between
Austria and Bavaria and the formation of a Danubian State – and a
45 new-comer at the back of the room. Then Feder seemed to grip
the audience. He had something very interesting to say about the
difference between loan (or unproductive) capital, and industrial
capital which feeds productive industry.'
  'I had been much struck by the objector from the back. He
50 spoke uncommonly well, and used his arguments with force as
telling as a flail. He seemed to know his ground, too, better than
most. I thought to myself "Herr Gott! here's a chap worth getting
hold of!" I kept an eye on him and when the meeting broke up,
made a bee-line for him just as he was leaving. I gave him a copy
55 of my pamphlet – asked him to come again – hoped he'd read it –
"AND THAT MAN WAS ADOLF HITLER".'

> Heinz a Heinz, *Germany's Hitler* (London, Hurst and
> Blackett, 1934), p 42

Questions

a   Who was Drexler trying to appeal to with his party?
b   Why do you think the German Workers' Party had only a
    limited success under Drexler?
★ c   Why did Hitler join this party?
d   This interview dates from 1934. In what ways does it appear
    rather melodramatic and why might it not be a completely
    true account of Drexler's feelings towards Hitler?

3   Early ideas of the Nazi Party

(a) The 25 Points

The Programme of the Party
  The Programme of the German Workers' Party is limited as to
period. The leaders have no intention, once the aims announced in
it have been achieved, of setting up fresh ones in order to ensure
the continued existence of the Party by the artificially increased
5 discontent of the masses.
    1. We demand the union of all Germans, on the basis of the right
      of the self-determination of peoples, to form a Great Germany.

2. We demand equality of rights for the German People in its dealings with other nations, and abolition of the Peace Treaties of Versailles and St. Germain.

3. We demand land and territory (colonies) for the nourishment of our people and for settling our surplus population.

4. None but members of the nation may be citizens of the State. None but those of German blood, whatever their creed, may be members of the nation. No Jew, therefore, may be a member of the nation.

5. Anyone who is not a citizen of the State may live in Germany only as a guest and must be regarded as being subject to the Alien laws.

6. The right of voting on the leadership and legislation is to be enjoyed by the citizens of the State alone. We demand, therefore, that all official appointments, of whatever kind, whether in the Reich, the provinces, or the small communities, shall be granted to citizens of the State alone.

   We oppose the corrupt Parliamentary custom of the State of filling posts merely with a view to Party considerations, and without reference to character or capacity.

7. We demand that the State shall make it its first duty to promote the industry and livelihood of the citizens of the State. If it is not possible to nourish the entire population of the State, foreign nationals (non-citizens of the State) must be excluded from the Reich.

8. All further non-German immigration must be prevented. We demand that all non-Germans who entered Germany subsequently to August 2, 1914, shall be required forthwith to depart from the Reich.

9. All citizens of the State shall possess equal rights and duties.

10. It must be the first duty of every citizen of the State to perform mental or physical work. The activities of the individual must not clash with the interests of the whole, but must proceed within the framework of the community and must be for the general good.

We demand therefore:

11. Abolition of incomes unearned by work. Abolition of the thraldom of interest.

12. In view of the enormous sacrifice of life and property demanded of a nation by every ward, personal enrichment through war must be regarded as a crime against the nation. We demand therefore the ruthless confiscation of all war profits.

13. We demand the nationalization of all businesses which have (hitherto) been amalgamated (into Trusts).

14. We demand that there shall be profit-sharing in the great industries.
15. We demand a general development of provision for old age.
16. We demand the creation and maintenance of a healthy middle class, immediate communalization of wholesale warehouses, and their lease at a low rate to small traders, and that the most careful consideration shall be shown to all small purveyors to the State, the provinces, or smaller communities.
17. We demand a land-reform suitable to our national requirements, the passing of a law for the confiscation without compensation of land for communal purposes, the abolition of interest on mortgages, and prohibition of all speculation in land. . . .
25. That all the foregoing requirements may be realized we demand the creation of a strong central power of the Reich, unconditional authority of the politically central Parliament over the entire Reich and its organization in general.

The formation of Diets and vocational Chambers for the purposes of executing the general laws promulgated by the Reich in the various States of the Confederation.

The leaders of the Party swear to proceed regardless of consequences – if necessary at the sacrifice of their lives – towards the fulfilment of the foregoing Points.

Munich, February 24, 1920.

N. Baynes (trans. and ed.), *The Speeches of Adolf Hitler (1922–1939)*, vol 1 (London, Oxford University Press, 1942) pp 102–107

(b) A cynical view

I remember one of my first conversations with him. It was nearly our first quarrel.

'Power!' screamed Adolf. 'We must have power!' 'Before we gain it,' I replied firmly, 'let us decide what we propose to do with it. Our programme is too vague; we must construct something solid and enduring.'

Hitler, who even then could hardly bear contradiction, thumped the table and barked:- 'Power first! Afterwards we can act as circumstances dictate!'

O. Strasser, *Hitler and I* (London, Jonathan Cape, 1940), p 42

(c) An outsider's view

'German Socialism – Adolf Hitler's Socialism – is a totally different thing from what is generally understood by this term, from the Socialism derived from Marxian and Communistic theory. The

first essential difference between the two consists in this, that the
90 former is strictly national in aim, scope and limit: the latter is
international without boundaries of race or land. The second vital
distinction is that the first has been set up by the wish of the
people concerned, the second is imposed upon nations by the will
of those who organise and propagate it. A third contrast can be
95 drawn insomuch as German Socialism tends to draw all sections
of the nation closely together, international socialism initiates class
war. German Socialism is directed by the country's nationals;
international socialism is an instrument of the Jews. In the former
it is the personality of the leader which tells; in the latter we have
100 nothing but the inertia of the mass which is exploited by the
organisers.'

> Heinz a Heinz, *Germany's Hitler* (London, Hurst and
> Blackett, 1934), p 54

Questions

a   According to the Programme (extract *a*) what were the Nazis'
     views on: (i) foreign policy; (ii) the economy; (iii) the role of
     the State?
b   What overtones of racism can you find in this Programme?
c   Who do you think might be attracted by the policies set out in
     this Programme?
d   Comment on Strasser's view in extract *b* 'Our programme is
     too vague; we must construct something solid and enduring'
     (lines 81–2).
e   Otto Strasser fell out with Hitler in 1930. Why might extract *b*
     be treated with some suspicion by historians?
★ f How accurate a summary of Nazi beliefs is extract *c*? Why is it
     difficult to define exactly what the Nazis stood for? Why is the
     25 Point Programme of only limited value?

4   The First Supporters

(a) A supporter from the workers

"After the Revolt in 1918 I was a Communist. I couldn't see any
other way to bring the sort of Socialism about that we wanted.
They'd always been painting the future so rosy what with their
'Life in beauty and worthiness'. And nothing has come of it. It
5 wasn't what you could rightly call a Revolution in 1918, only a lot
of places emptied to be filled up with nincompoops with no idea
in their heads but to fill their own stomachs, and to have a good
time themselves. They forgot all about us workers. The only
people we've got any use for is those what don't confine

themselves to words, but who go and do something! That sort of thing turned me Communist.

"Then in 1921 or thereabouts everyone in Munich seemed to be talking about some new Party or other here what called itself 'Nationalist'. The name alone was enough to make us hate it. Not that I worried myself much about it at first. Never give it a thought, until one day some of our chaps turned up in the factory with their heads in bandages. At first they wouldn't let on what had happened, only mumbled something and turned aside. But it must have been pretty lively, that scrap, the way them chaps seemed to have got it in the neck! It all came out of course, sooner or later. A hundred or more of them had made it up together to go to one of this new Party's meetings and smash it up. They hadn't succeeded.

"I couldn't rightly believe my ears when I heard as it was only a handful of fellows at the meeting as had chucked them out. But everybody was talking of it. It was a sort of sensation for a day or two in Munich.

"That attracted my attention. I thought I'd go and have a look in at the next meeting of these here Nationalists.

"I stuck myself in a corner and kept my eyes and ears well open. The first thing I seemed to notice was that this wasn't no mere 'bourgeois' gathering, and no 'high-brow' one either. The audience was made up of plain folk like myself, working men and petty shopkeepers.

"Then this man Hitler got up to speak . . . .

"I saw at once this wasn't no common or garden tubthumper, no gasbag like the most of them. Everything he said was just common sense and sound. Although I wasn't one to be won over all in a moment, it didn't take me no longer than that first meeting to realise that Hitler was straight as a die, and a safe one to put your shirt on.

"I went to every one of his meetings after that. Bit by bit he won me round. He got in blow after blow at all the ideas I'd been holding on to up to now and laid them out flat! He knocked the Red nonsense out of me – all about the World Revolution to put the world right, and hot air like that. Instead, I seemed to see what he was driving at. Instead of prophecies and far-off Utopias like, in National Socialism, he gave us a good working scheme of things we could busy on right away.

"The first thing for me to do was to break with the Communists. So I did, and in the spring of 1922 I joined Hitler's Party. They shoved me into the guard straight away, the Storm Troops they were called, whose job it was to keep order at the meetings.

Heinz a Heinz, *Germany's Hitler* (London, Hurst and Blackett, 1934), p 126–7

(b) One of Hitler's friends

I cannot have been more than eight feet away and watched him
carefully. For the first ten minutes he stood at attention while he
gave a very well argued résumé of the historical events of the
previous three or four years. In a quiet, reserved voice, he drew a
picture of what had happened in Germany since November 1918:
the collapse of the monarchy and the surrender at Versailles; the
founding of the Republic on the ignomy of war guilt; the fallacy
of international Marxism and Pacifism; the eternal class war
leitmotif and the resulting hopeless stalemate between employers
and employees, between Nationalists and Socialists.

> E. Hanfstaengl, *Hitler, The Missing Years* (London, Eyre
> and Spottiswoode, 1957), p 34

(c) Albert Speer, Hitler's architect

Here, it seemed to me, was hope. Here were new ideals, a new
understanding, new tasks. Even Spengler's dark predictions
seemed to me refuted, and his prophecy of the coming of a new
Roman emperor simultaneously fulfilled. The peril of communism,
which seemed inexorably on its way, could be checked, Hitler
persuaded us, and instead of hopeless unemployment, Germany
could move toward economic recovery. He had mentioned the
Jewish problem only peripherally. But such remarks did not
worry me, although I was not an anti-Semite; rather, I had Jewish
friends from my school days and university days, like virtually
everyone else.

> A. Speer, *Inside the Third Reich* (London, Weidenfeld and
> Nicolson, 1970), p 46

Questions

a   How did the interviewee in extract *a* come to hear of the Nazi
party? Why did he go along to a meeting?

★ b   Why did the interviewee join the Nazi party? What does this
account show about the differences and similarities between
the Nazi and Communist parties?

c   How positive is Hitler's speech as summarised in extract *b*?

d   Speer's book was published long after the war. What aspects of
extract *c* could be seen as a form of excuse for his behaviour?

e   Compare the three extracts. In what ways do the listeners vary
in their response to Hitler's speeches?

★ f   On the basis of these extracts and other sources, why was
Hitler so effective as a public speaker? In what other ways did
he spread the Nazi message during these early years?

★   *g*   Find out about Hitler's early followers (their backgrounds, service in World War I, their role in the Nazi party): (i) Ernst Röhm; (ii) Alfred Rosenberg; (iii) Rudolf Hess; (iv) Herman Goering. Why do you think each of them supported the Nazi party?

5   The S.A

(a) Hitler's view

But the success of this first larger meeting was also important from another point of view. I had already begun to introduce some young and fresh members into the committee. During the long period of my military service I had come to know a large
5   number of good comrades whom I was now able to persuade to join our party. All of them were energetic and disciplined young men who, through their years of military service, had been imbued with the principle that nothing is impossible and that where there's a will there's a way.

> A. Hitler, *Mein Kampf* (London, Hurst and Blackett, 1939), p 298

(b) A storm-trooper's account

10   'At the end of August 1922,' continues Herr Schmitt, 'there was to be a big meeting held by some of the societies in the city to protest against a new law which had been passed in protection of the Republic. Hitler thought it an A1 opportunity to bring his troopers for the first time into the open, and to give Munich an
15   idea of their strength and discipline. We were six companies (600) strong by then, we had 15 flags and two bands. We turned out and marched with music at the head of the column into the Konigsplatz where the meeting was to come off. At first we encountered little that was unpleasant. They flung a few stones at
20   us from some of the side streets, but we was under strict orders to take no notice of such petty manoeuvres, so we kept straight on. But then things got a bit livelier. Just before we reached the square Hitler right about faced and gave the signal to clear the streets. We flung ourselves upon our attackers, and with two shakes of a
25   lamb's tail there wasn't a man left of them to be seen. And in the Konigsplatz itself we got a downright ovation. The people hadn't seen anything like us for our formation, flags and bands, for ages. A crowd of 40,000 greeted our appearance.'

> Heinz a Heinz, *Germany's Hitler* (London, Hurst and Blackett, 1934), p 168

a In what ways did Hitler try to attract the young to the Nazi party, as suggested by extract a?

b Read the storm-trooper's account in extract b. How might this event impress onlookers and lead people to join the Nazi party?

c It was claimed by some Nazi apologists that the S.A. was set up purely for defensive purposes at party meetings. How far does extract b support this view?

★ d How useful was the S.A. to the Nazi party? What drawbacks did it have?

6 The Munich Putsch

(a) Hitler's hopes

Already in the summer it was clear to us that on one side or the other in Germany the die must be cast. We felt at the time that we, although perhaps in numbers the weakest of the parties, were worth more than all the others. In the autumn when events
5 crowded one upon another, it became even clearer that under the pressure of the occupation of the Ruhr certain unscrupulous scoundrels were trying to tear Germany asunder. There then grew amongst us, I may say with me, the determination that, if it should really come to this pass, then at least twenty-four hours
10 before that step was taken we should seize the initiative and would not wait until the other side should perhaps discover the courage to make up their minds – and to act. For one thing was clear; he who, in the inflation period, in this time of collapse of everything and everyone, had the courage to come to a decision – he would
15 have the people behind him.'

N. Baynes (trans. and ed.), *The Speeches of Adolf Hitler (1922–1939)*, vol 1 (London, Oxford University Press, 1942), p 120

(b) Other pressures

At the trial after the Putsch, the commander of the Munich S.A. regiment said:

'I had the impression that the Reichswehr officers were dissatisfied too, because the march on Berlin was being held up.
20 They were saying: Hitler is a fraud just like the rest of them. You are not attacking. It makes no difference to us who strikes first; we are going along! And I myself told Hitler: "One of these days I will not be able to hold the men back. Unless something happens now, the men will take off on you!" We had many unemployed in

25 the ranks, fellows who had sacrificed their last pair of shoes, their
last suit of clothing, their last penny for their training and who
thought: "soon things will get under way and we'll be taken into the
Reichswehr and be out of this mess".'

> Quoted in J. Fest, *Hitler* (London, Weidenfeld and Nicolson,
> 1974), pp 179–80

Questions

a   In extract *a* who, supposedly, were the 'certain unscrupulous
     scoundrels trying to tear Germany asunder' (lines 6–7)?

★   b   Why had Hitler taken the decision by autumn 1924 to launch a
         Putsch? Did he 'have the people behind him' (line 15)?

c   What types of people joined the S.A., according to extract *b*?

★   d   The author of extract *b* claimed support for the S.A. from the
         army (Reichswehr). What evidence is there in this extract
         and elsewhere to support or refute this view with regard to the
         Munich Putsch?

e   Why does Hitler make no reference to the feelings of the S.A
     in his explanation for beginning the Putsch?

(c) The reluctant conspirators: the beer-hall Putsch

The crowd began to break up. The agitated human stress seeped
slowly through the narrow door. Most felt exalted and happy, a
few dubious and worried; all were moved by the feeling that they
had experienced a bit of history behind their beer mugs. Lossow
5 nonchalantly [sic] informed Ludendorff that he was going to his
office, as there were important orders to be given. With Kahr and
Seisser, he vanished in the departing crowd. 'Is it safe to let them
go?' Scheubner-Richter whispered to Ludendorff. 'I forbid you to
doubt the word of a German officer,' Ludendorff replied sharply.
10 In the vestibule one of Kahr's officials approached and asked what
all this meant? The little dictator replied: 'Herr Kollega, I am
really despondent. You yourself saw that I was forced to give my
consent. That kind of thing simply isn't done.'

> K. Heiden, *Hitler, A Biography* (New York, Alfred A.
> Knopf, 1936), p 130

(d) The next day

An hour before midnight, Hitler appeared at the War Ministry
15 and embraced Captain Roehm.

   'This is the happiest and most wonderful day of my life,' he
said, glowing, apparently all unaware of signs of impending disaster.
'Now we shall see better times – we will all work, day and night,
towards our great goal – to rescue Germany from her misery and
20 disgrace.'

As the night wore on, Ludendorff and Kriebel, waiting at the
War Ministry, began to have misgivings, and sent several officers
in turn to Lossow to find out what was going on. They did not
return; each of them had been arrested on the spot. Then, at
25 dawn, Poehner was roused from his bed to inform himself of the
situation. Accompanied by Major Huehnlein, he went to police
headquarters, and they also were arrested.

Finally, in the early morning, Ludendorff and Kriebel joined
Hitler at the Burgerbraukeller. Still no news from Kahr, Lossow
30 or Seisser. Hitler and Ludendorff at last were realising that
something had gone amiss.

. . . Morning still found the Landspolizei or state police still
with Hitler and Ludendorff. The morning papers lauded the
national revolution enthusiastically hailing the turn of events and
35 Hitler's proclamation as though the new order had come to stay.
The offices of the Marxian 'Muenchener Post' were demolished;
the political bosses of the Marxian parties were placed under arrest
and ordered shot. No one outside the immediate entourage of
Hitler and Ludendorff knew how seriously the situation was now
40 going against them. Even Hitler and two thousand S.A. men who
had received rifles from a secret depot were unaware that the
firing pins, ordinarily removed to prevent misuse of the weapons,
had not been replaced; in an encounter they would have been
completely worthless.
45 . . . The council in the Burgerbraukeller had become gloomier
and gloomier. A hundred plans were discussed and discarded –
among them, the desperate coup of storming the Reichswehr
barracks before they could be reinforced. It would have been
madness, for the Kampfbund was no match for regular troops
50 with armoured cars, light artillery, gas and all the paraphernalia of
war.

Finally Ludendorff's advice prevailed, and it was decided to
march into Munich. Counting on a huge popular demonstration
in their favour, they hoped that with tens of thousands of burghers
55 marching behind them through the heart of the city the Reichswehr
and police would refuse to fire. The situation might be carried,
after all, by the strength of the almost unanimous sympathy and
enthusiasm of the people for the 'national revolution'. Streicher,
Esser and other speakers were sent out to whip up the populace to
60 a favourable response.

> K. Ludecke, *I Knew Hitler* (London, Jarrolds, 1938), p 58

Questions

★ a Who were the following: (i) Lossow; (ii) Kahr; (iii) Seisser;
(iv) Ludendorff?

 b In extract *b* why did Kahr, Lossow and Seisser leave the meeting?

Why does the extract lay stress on the fact that Ludendorff did not stop them?

c What part did Kahr play in the Putsch? What was the meaning of his comment, 'That kind of thing simply isn't done' (line 13)?

d How did the mood change during the day as described in extract *d*?

e How big a role did Hitler seem to play in the Putsch according to extracts *c* and *d*?

★ f Why did the Putsch fail to attract much support?

(e) The trial

On the one side an act of high treason had been committed against the country openly and shamelessly. On the other side a nation found itself delivered over to die slowly of hunger. Since the State itself had trodden down all the precepts of faith and loyalty, made
5 a mockery of the rights of its citizens, rendered the sacrifices of millions of its most loyal sons fruitless and robbed other millions of their last penny, such a state could no longer expect anything but hatred from its subjects. This hatred against those who had ruined the people and the country was bound to find a outlet in
10 one form or another. In this connection I shall quote here the concluding sentence in a speech which I delivered at the great court trial that took place in the spring of 1924.

'The judges of this state may tranquilly condemn us for our conduct at that time; but History, the goddess of a higher truth
15 and a better legal code, will smile as she tears up this verdict and will acquit us all of the crime for which this verdict demands punishment.'

A. Hitler, *Mein Kampf* (London, Hurst and Blackett, 1939), p 220

(f) Explanations

It was the greatest good fortune for us National Socialists that the Putsch collapsed, because:-
20 1. Cooperation with General Ludendorff would have been absolutely impossible . . . .
2. The sudden takeover of power in the whole of Germany would have led to the greatest of difficulties in 1923 because the essential preparations had not been even begun by the
25 National Socialist Party and
3. The events of 9 November 1923 in front of the Feldeherrnhalle, with their blood sacrifice, have proven to be the most effective propaganda for National Socialism.

Hitler in 1933, quoted in W. Gordon, *The Munich Putsch* (Princetown, New York, Bernard and Graefe, 1978), p 190

(g) Afterthoughts

30 'I was following Mussolini's example too closely,' the Chancellor told me twelve years after the event. 'I had meant the Munich Putsch to be the beginning of a "March on Berlin" which should carry us straight to power. From its failure I learnt the lesson that each country must evolve its own type and methods of national regeneration.'

> G. Ward Price, *I Know these Dictators* (London, Harrap, 1939), p 79

Questions

a   Why did Hitler claim in extract *e* that 'the goddess of a higher truth . . . will acquit us all of the crime . . .' (lines 14–17)?

★ b   How did Hitler make use of the trial? Why did he take all the blame himself?

c   How credible do you find Hitler's explanations as set out in extract *f*?

★ d   Why did the 'March on Berlin' fail and the March on Rome succeed?

★ e   What effect did the Munich Putsch have on the Nazi party?

II Reorganisation and Breakthrough 1925–30

Introduction

After Hitler was released from jail in December 1924 there was a reassessment of Nazi policy. The aim was still to take over the state but now by legal means and by using the methods of the state itself. As Hitler relates, this appeared not to be easy to get over to some traditional Nazi supporters and there were further problems with the more radical Nazis, especially the Strasser brothers. Whether the clash was between ideologies or personalities it is difficult to say. Either way, the socialist Nazis did not disappear, but Hitler did reassert his authority.

Perhaps of even more importance at this period was the careful build up of Nazi organisations. Nationwide party cells, groups associated with all aspects of society – teachers, students, women – and a variety of insignia and displays contributed to the creation of a party with the potential to cope with a vast increase in numbers: but for most of this period the German economy continued to do well and the Nazis remained a party in the wings with support from only the lower middle class and, latterly, the farmers.

External events now came to the assistance of the Nazis. A new reparations scheme, the Young plan, provoked further fury from the right wing. Hitler found himself in alliance with Alfred Hugenburg, a rich magnate and newspaper owner with his own relatively small party, the D.N.V.P. Whatever the alliance did for Hugenburg, it is usually argued that Hitler benefited more; he gained money, publicity and a veneer of respectability.

This was not a permanent alliance, nor does it appear to have found favour with all members of the Nazi party: once again, Hitler appeared to have been going his own way. But the broad links were already established when the Wall Street Crash of 1929 led to economic disaster for Germany. The Weimar government's seeming inability to cope with the crisis gave the opportunity for new parties to make their mark. Quite why the public – or a sizeable proportion of them – chose to vote for the Nazis, a known racist and aggressive party, is difficult to answer. Whatever the reasons, in the September elections of 1930 the Nazis finally achieved their breakthrough and became a major party.

1   The Legal Approach

'From now on,' he said 'we must follow a new line of action. It is best to attempt no large reorganisation until I am freed, which may be a matter of months rather than of years.'

I must have looked at him somewhat incredulously. 'Oh, yes,'
5 he continued. 'I am not going to stay here much longer. When I resume active work it will be necessary to pursue a new policy. Instead of working to achieve power by an armed coup, we shall have to hold our noses and enter the Reichstag against the Catholic and Marxist deputies. If out-voting them takes longer than
10 outshooting them, at least the results will be guaranteed by their own Constitution! Any lawful process is slow. But already, as you know, we have thirty-two Reichstag deputies under this new programme, and are the second largest Party in the Bavarian Landtag-diet. Sooner or later we shall have a majority – and after
15 that, Germany. I am convinced this is our best line of action, now that conditions in the country have changed so radically.'

I was not a little surprised to hear the Führer talking this way. Only a few weeks earlier he had voiced through Esser and Streicher his violent opposition to any participation in the May
20 elections, and had raged when Party members had entered as candidates despite his ban. I could not then see into Hitler's mind. Twelve years of hindsight, however, are better than one flash of clairvoyance.

Leaving Hitler for the moment still seated across the table in
25 Landsberg, let me try to set forth his attitude at that time as I understand it now.

The unexpected success in the elections undoubtedly had swayed him. Probably more important was the fact that conditions had indeed altered. Most immediate and far-reaching of the changes
30 was the end of the inflation, which stopped just short of final chaos a few days after the putsch. Germany's new coin, the gold Renten mark, proved to be stable; . . . the sudden stabilization ended the general panic, and with it the illusory solidarity of the people. The Haves and Have-nots, renouncing the loose union
35 into which their common plight had forced them, now resumed their habitual antagonism. Thus, while the anti-capitalist sentiment which Hitler had orchestrated was intensified in some quarters, better economic conditions were robbing the tune of its mass appeal, and he could no longer count on wooing the mob with it.
40 As for the desperate remedies by which he had proposed to cure the other national ills, it was best for a while to advocate less violent measures. As long as the crisis had remained desperate, a great part of the nation had endorsed direct action; but now that the danger appeared less imminent, he would find only scattered
45 support.

Moreover, on account of his absence from the platform and the Party's dissolution through official decree, there could be no hope of renewing the struggle along the old lines. Though Hitler's well-publicised forensics at the court trial had repaired most of the damage, Nazi prestige had suffered after the putsch, the National Socialist German Workers' Party remained under a legal ban. Technically it was dead as a door nail.

> K. Ludecke, *I Knew Hitler* (London, Jarrolds, 1938), pp 217–19

Questions

★ *a* Why, according to Ludecke, did Hitler change to a legal approach? What other reasons were there for this change of policy? What effects do you think the Putsch had on this change?

★ *b* How did the Ruhr crisis come to an end? What was the 'Renten mark' (line 32) and what was its importance?

c Comment on the statement: 'Hitlers well-publicised forensics at the court trial had repaired most of the damage' (lines 48–50).

d Why was Hitler at Landsberg? What does his claim about only being there for a short time reveal about the political beliefs of the local, Bavarian government?

★ *e* What happened to the Nazi party while Hitler was in jail?

★ *f* Why did the Nazis gain relatively few votes in national elections between 1924–28?

2 Party Dissension

(a) The Strasser's programme

Our second step was to work out an economic, political and cultural programme. In the economic field it was opposed alike to Marxism and capitalism. We foresaw a new equilibrium on a basis of state feudalism. The State was to be the sole owner of the land, which it would lease to private citizens. All were to be free to do as they liked with their own land, but no one could sell or sub-let state property. In this way we hoped to combat proletarianization and to restore a sense of liberty to our fellow-citizens. No man is free who is not economically independent.

We proposed nationalization only of such wealth as could not be multiplied at will, i.e. the country's landed and industrial inheritance.

In the political field we rejected the totalitarian idea in favour of federalism. Parliament, instead of consisting of party representatives, would consist of representatives of corporations. These we divided into five groups; workers, peasants, clerks and

officials, industrialists, and the liberal professions. Politically
Germany would be decentralized and divided into cantons on the
Swiss model. Prussia, separated from the Rhineland from Hesse,
20 Hanover, Saxony and Schleswig-Holstein, would lose her
hegemony and cease to exist. The administration of each canton,
from the governor to the humblest porter, would be exclusively
in the hands of natives of the canton.

The prosperity of the country would be assured by the
25 nationalization of heavy industry and the distribution of the great
estates as state fiefs.

Our programme foresaw the destruction of Prussian militarism.
Under a new Constitution there would be either a small
professional army or a militia on Swiss lines.
30 In the field of foreign politics we naturally demanded equality
between the nations, and the cessation of the ostracism of Germany
that still prevailed. We had no territorial demands, looking
forward at most to the holding of honest plebiscites in disputed
areas.
35 A European federation, based on the same principle as those of
federal Germany, would lead to a disarmed Europe, forming a
solid bloc in which each country retained its own administration,
customs and religion. The abolition of tariff walls would create a
kind of European Autarkie, with Free Trade prevailing throughout
40 the Continent. This would be as desirable in the economic as in
the cultural field.

O. Strasser, *Hitler and I* (London, Jonathan Cape, 1940),
pp 92–3

(b) The Hanover meeting

When all was in readiness Gregor called a meeting of the regional
leaders of Hanover under our joint presidency. The Gauleiters of
the North answered his call; Kaufmann, Rust, now Reich Minister
45 of Education; Kerrl, present Minister of Ecclesiastical Affairs; Ley,
leader of the Labour Front, and Hildebrandt, the present Governor
of Mecklenburg. There were about twenty-four of us, and our
number was completed by Gottfried Feder, Hitler's deputy.

When the northern leaders learned that Hitler proposed to be
50 represented at Hanover there was great indignation.

'No spies in our midst!' exclaimed Goebbels, always more
royalist than the King.

The motion that Feder should be admitted to the meeting was
put to the vote and passed by a bare majority.
55 A problem of the greatest importance was raised at this
conference.

The whole country was divided on the question of the
expropriation of the German royal houses.

The inflation period was fortunately over, and the mark had
been stabilized, but War Loan subscribers could not be repaid and
the small rentiers were not drawing a farthing. In these
circumstances was it not immoral to restore to the princes, the
men responsible for the war and its consequences, their castles,
their lands and something like a hundred million gold marks? The
working-class parties and the German democrats were violently
opposed to the measure, and the National-Socialist Party of the
North seemed equally opposed. In anticipation of this first German
plebiscite our leaders were anxious to pass a resolution on the
subject, and Feder's presence was embarrassing. Daily reports
from Bavaria told us which way Adolf was moving, and we were
perfectly well aware that a National-Socialist vote in favour of
expropriation would be at complete variance with his new tactics.

At Hanover everyone except Dr. Ley voted for it. When Feder
protested in Hitler's name Goebbels leapt to his feet and made a
passionate speech in our support.

'In these circumstances I demand that the petty bourgeois Adolf
Hitler be expelled from the National-Socialist Party,' he thundered.
I may add that he was loudly applauded.

Gregor had to intervene firmly and point out that such a
decision could only be taken by a general Party Congress. In any
case it was agreed that the National-Socialist Party of the North
would vote against the princes.

'The National-Socialists are free and democratic men,' Rust
ardently declared. 'They have no pope who can claim infallibility.
Hitler can act as he likes, but we shall act according to our
conscience.'

O. Strasser, *Hitler and I* (London, Jonathan Cape, 1940),
pp 96–7

(c) Defeat at Bamberg

As soon as Hitler had finished, Josef Goebbels, spokesman of the
National-Socialist Party of the North and Gregor Strasser's private
secretary, rose to his feet.

'Herr Adolf Hitler is right,' he declared (the word 'Führer' had
not yet been introduced into the Nazi vocabulary). 'His arguments
are so convincing that there is no disgrace in admitting our
mistakes and rejoining him.'

No one in the Party has forgotten Goebbels' unspeakable
conduct. Veterans talk of 'the traitor of Bamberg' to this day.

Hitler seemed to have anticipated the little cripple's volte-face,
and to have decided that Gregor Strasser, separated from his
associates, isolated in a hostile congress and facing a bitter defeat,
would be in no position to resist him.

A battle-royal between Adolf and Gregor inevitably ensued

next day. So terrific was the debate between them that at times Gregor felt it was more like hand-to-hand fighting.

'I defended our position vigorously,' he told me, 'but I could feel that Adolf was gaining ground. He was rarely violent, but he called on all the generosity and all the arts of seduction of which he is master. Once or twice he came close to me, and I thought he was going to seize me by the throat, but instead he put his arm around my shoulders and talked to me like a friend. 'Listen, Strasser', he said, 'you really mustn't go on living like a wretched official. Sell your pharmacy, draw on the Party funds and set yourself up properly as a man of your worth should.'

I listened to Gregor's story with growing misgivings, knowing only too well which way Adolf Hitler was going. He was trying to turn Gregor into a docile instrument like the rest, a slave of the funds that he had amassed.

The compromise that resulted from this oratorical clash between Hitler and Gregor was not entirely disastrous to us. We retained our independence, the right to run our publishing house and to publish the Nationalsozialistische Briefe. On the other hand we had to renounce our programme and adhere once more to Hitler's Twenty-Five Points.

'Above all,' I counselled Gregor, 'keep your pharmacy and don't take any of his money.'

O. Strasser, *Hitler and I* (London, Jonathan Cape, 1940), pp 100–101

(d) *Hitler on party leadership*

The greatest danger that can threaten a movement is an abnormal increase in the number of its members, owing to its too rapid success. So long as a movement has to carry on a hard and bitter fight, people of weak and fundamentally egotistic temperament will steer very clear of it; but these will try to be accepted as members the moment the party achieves a manifest success in the course of its development.

It is on these grounds that we are to explain why so many movements which were at first successful slowed down before reaching the fulfilment of their purpose and, from an inner weakness which could not otherwise be explained, gave up the struggle and finally disappeared from the field. As a result of the early successes achieved, so many undesirable, unworthy and especially timid individuals became members of the movement that they finally secured the majority and stifled the fighting spirit of the others.

For this reason it is necessary that a movement should, from the sheer instinct of self-preservation, close its lists to new membership the moment it becomes successful. . . . Care must be taken that

the conduct of the movement is maintained exclusively in the
hands of this original nucleus. . . .

45   The problem of the inner organisation of the movement is not
one of principle but of expediency.

The best kind of organisation is not that which places a large
intermediary apparatus between the leadership of the movement
and the individual followers but rather that which works
50 successfully with the smallest possible intermediary apparatus. For
it is the task of such an organisation to transmit a certain idea
which originated in the brain of one individual to a multitude of
people and to supervise the manner in which this idea is being put
into practice.

> A. Hitler, *Mein Kampf* (London, Hurst and Blackett, 1939),
> pp 477, 290

Questions

a   What does Strasser mean in extract *a* when he refers to his
policies as 'state feudalism' (line 4)? How radical were these
policies?

b   Compare the Strasser policies with Hitler's 25 Points (Ch 1,
pp 9–11). In what ways are they different? Are they
incompatible?

c   According to extract *b*, what event led to an open split with
Hitler?

d   In what ways does extract *b* attempt to show that Hitler was
treated fairly? Why do you think the account is written in this
way?

★ e   How did Hitler defeat the Strasser brothers?

f   What attitude does Strasser adopt towards Goebbels in extract
c and why?

g   What do these extracts show about the organisation of the
Nazi party? On what terms did similar right-wing groups join
with Hitler's party? Why do you think other groups would
join together?

h   What does extract *d* reveal about Hitler's attitude towards the
role of the party and the leadership principle?

3   Party Organisation

Never has any Party prepared for power more thoroughly than
the Nazis during the eight years between Hitler's release from
Landsberg and his arrival at the Chancellorship. Their campaign
was by no means confined to speeches and propaganda, though
5 these were poured out in constantly increasing volume. With
German zest for organisation the framework of the Nazi movement

was expanded and departmentalized until it had virtually became a 'shadow Government'.

It had its 'Cabinet', consisting of Hitler and his intimate advisers; a political department, with sub-divisions gradually extending throughout the country; a Press and propaganda organisation; and bureaux for dealing with labour questions, agricultural interests, and financial matters.

There were technical corps for the Party's motor and aerial transport; supply-services which passed large contracts for uniforms, banners and Party equipment; an insurance fund for the dependents of members killed or injured in clashes with the Communists. A legal branch conducted the law-suits in which the Party was frequently involved, and lastly, the defence departments of an actual Government were represented by the Storm Troopers and the 'Protection Guards' organised on military lines under their commanding officers, Ernst Röhm and Heinrich Himmler.

G. Ward Price, *I Know these Dictators* (London, Harrap, 1937), p 91

Questions

a What sort of shadow government was set up by the Nazi party during this period?

b What use did this type of organisation have at this time? Why was it particularly useful when the party began to expand in later years?

★ *c* By what means did the Nazis spread their beliefs at this time?

4 The Young Plan and The Hugenberg Alliance

(a) An industrialist's misgivings

I turned to the National Socialist party only after I became convinced that the fight against the Young Plan was unavoidable if a complete collapse of Germany was to be prevented. In no sense had I been an opponent of the Dawes Plan, since the Dawes Plan envisaged a system of reparation payments to be made chiefly in goods. But under the Young Plan the German reparation deliveries were superseded entirely by money payments. In my judgement the financial debt thus created was bound to disrupt the entire economy of the Reich. Walter Rathenau, too, had regarded this as a misfortune: he had always maintained the view that Germany could pay only in the goods it produced.

One of our representatives in the committee of experts which conducted the preliminary negotiations concerning the revision of the Dawes Plan in Paris was Director General Vögler, of the Gelsenkirchen iron and steel concern. These Paris negotiations

were interrupted, and both Vögler and Dr. Hjalmar Schacht, the
president of the Reichsbank, returned to Germany because they
had misgivings about the proposed Plan. In the end, too, Vögler
did not sign the new proposals which became the basis of the
20 Young Plan; and I must admit that I had done all I could do to
convince him of the correctness of his misgivings. . . . Anybody
with the power of clear judgement saw that the Young Plan
meant the pledging of Germany's entire wealth as a pawn for
Germany's obligations.

    F. Thyssen, *I paid Hitler* (Port Washington, New York,
Kennikat Press, 1972), pp 88–9

(b) A minister's defence

25 Guilt lie. Every German Government, as also President von
Hindenburg and the Foreign Minister, Dr. Stresemann, have
indignantly repudiated the assertion that Germany was responsible
for the World War. The campaign against this guilt lie will be
carried on by the whole nation and by the appropriate Departments
30 of State with all available resources. In provoking a campaign
against the War Guilt lie, the Hugenburg Plebiscite is pushing at
an open door. But in doing so it attempts to give the impression
that a law passed in Germany can invalidate international treaties,
it is suggesting to the German people a possibility which, as the
35 originator of the proposal knows, unfortunately does not exist.

    The point at issue is the continuance of the policy which began
with the Dawes Plan, with the object of lightening the obligations
for which, as a result of the lost War, despite the resistance of the
German Peoples Party, at Versailles and on the occasions of the
40 London ultimatum, German signatures have already been given.

    Do not the advocates of the plebiscite also see the significance of
the Young Plan is not exhausted by the material provisions, but
that its outstanding achievement is the final liberation from foreign
occupation and the abolition of the control system which was so
45 repugnant to every German feeling?

    To threaten the men who strained all their energies and sacrificed
their health in this war of liberation with the accusation of treason
is an infamy for which the bitterest political struggle can offer no
excuse.

    E. Sutton (ed.), *Gustav Stresemann – Diaries, Letters and
Papers*, vol 1 (London, Macmillan, 1935), p 127

(c) The Hugenberg Alliance

50 Hitler began to see that in this struggle, if he insisted on marching
separately, he would be left without resources. He journeyed to
Berlin and met Hugenberg in the premises of the Deutscher

Orden, a sort of nationalist lodge. Again the case of Strasser came up for discussion. There was also talk of Gottfried Feder. Hitler himself was beginning at this time to regard his economic prophet as the dilettante which Goebbels had always pronounced him. Hitler promised that the attacks on industry would cease in future if industry would champion the national war of liberation. But that it was doing at this moment; Hugenberg was sitting there as the embodiment of the new political aspirations of industry. Hitler was ready to believe this and to confirm this belief by joining Hugenberg's Committee of Action. He made the condition, however, that outwardly his party should be completely independent and should wage the struggle for the common aim in its own way. That, for this purpose, it would need a very large portion of the available monetary resources went without saying; in order that this condition might be strictly fulfilled, no other than Gregor Strasser would be National-Socialist member of the Finance Committee of the enterprise. Hugenberg was surprised at the selection of Gregor Strasser, but Hitler was sure of his subordinate leader.

While hardly a soul in the party suspected anything, Hitler made a surprise appearance in Berlin and spoke at a small private demonstration against the Young Plan organised by Hugenberg. The National-Socialist Reichstag group now learned for the first time of its German Nationalist colleague: Your chief is here, they were told, and is showing himself to the people arm-in-arm with Hugenberg. They rushed to the meeting-hall in the former Upper House and reached it just in time to hear the conclusion of Hitler's speech. Great stupefaction among most of them. At length Lohse, the deputy, said: "One can only hope that the Führer knows already how he's going to bamboozle Hugenberg."

The Führer did know. He issued an order to the party: the ultimate aim of the party remains unaltered. Only orders of the party management are valid; joint demonstrations with other associations must be expressly allowed by the party administration. Later "in the free play of forces the clearest and boldest German movement will work its way through to final victory".

Thus did Hitler conclude alliances. Now he meant to show the German nationalists how to conduct propaganda! The whole campaign against the Young Plan was completely dominated by the National Socialists. Hugenberg's news bureaus had to give prominence to Hitler's speeches, for the newspapers in the country, which veered with every wind, demanded this; his own newspapers had to do the same, for the readers demanded it. And for all this Hugenberg had to pay. . . .

The referendum was an utter failure. The voice of the people was clearly in favour of the Young Plan. But it was Hugenberg who was beaten. Hitler had the money in his coffers and he knew that this six million who voted against the referendum included about three million who a year ago had still voted for Hugenberg and who were now won over to the National-Socialists.

K. Heiden, *A History of National Socialism* (London, Methuen, 1934), pp 230–1

Questions

a What were the Dawes and Young Plans (extract *a*)? Why did Thyssen support the first and yet oppose the second?

b Why was it important that people such as Thyssen joined the Nazi party?

c Why, in extract *b*, did Stresemann support the Young Plan? Why did he oppose the Hugenberg Plebiscite?

d Why did Hugenberg raise questions concerning Feder and Strasser (extract *c*)? Why were some Nazis surprised and reluctant to join with Hugenberg?

★ e To what extent was it true that 'it was Hugenberg who was beaten' (line 99)? Why did Hitler and Hugenberg form an alliance and who benefited the most from it?

5   The Breakthrough to Mass Support

(a) A Nazi appeal to the middle class

The middle-class parties pledged to save the Mittelstand from destruction, but it is rapidly nearing its utter demise! The revalorisation parties promised to introduce compensation for the crimes of the inflation. These parties live on, but the victims of the
5 inflation are slowly dying. The parties for the salvation of small business promise to help the small craftsmen, the shopkeeper, and merchant. But with their aid, the large department stores spring up and strangle hundreds of thousands of independent businessmen.

Article in the *Volkischer Beobachter*, 10 September 1930, quoted in T. Childers, *The Nazi Voter* (Chapel Hill and London, University of North Carolina Press, 1983)

(b) A middle-class Nazi

"At the end of my time at the university," he continued, "I was
10 unemployed for a year, so I went back to do some research work in the hope that perhaps times would improve. But for five years I remained unemployed and was broken in body and spirit and I learned how stupid were all my dreams in those hard days at the university. I was not wanted by Germany, and certainly if I was
15 not wanted here I was not wanted anywhere in the world. Even more futile were all our international youth movements, for the

League of Nations was not interested in peace, it was only
interested in maintaining the status quo, and it never had the
courage to put anything right in Europe. Heavens, how the
20   younger crowd were duped into false hopes for the future! At any
rate, life became for me completely hopeless.

"Just then I was introduced to Hitler. You won't understand
and I cannot explain either because I don't know what happened,
but life for me took on a tremendous new significance. After all,
25   Germany would rise again; after all, I was wanted. I have since
committed myself, body, soul and spirit, to this movement for
the resurrection of Germany. I can only tell you that I cannot go
back, I cannot question, I am pledged. I beg you not to try to set
up conflict in my mind. I dare not let that happen for I am as
30   much committed to Hitler as the fundamentalist is to his Bible.
Believe me, I cannot face uncertainty and conflict again. No, for
me it is Hitler and the resurrection of Germany on one side, or
suicide on the other.

"I have chosen Hitler, leave me in peace with my choice."

E. Buller, *Darkness over Germany* (London, Longmans,
Green and Co., 1941), p 108

(c) Nazi propaganda

35   A still greater impression was made on the electors by a brochure
that was published and circulated to the extent of sixty thousand
copies all over the country as the official 'Immediate Economic
Programme' of the National Socialist Party. This pamphlet, which
runs to thirty-two pages, will remain as a permanent record of
40   what unscrupulous propagandists will offer to a desperate people.
The first promise concerned the improvement of the soil, which
was to increase the annual yield from German arable land by two
milliards of Marks. What could the people think? Two milliards
more every year for German agriculture – and an evidently
45   criminal Government had hitherto neglected even to begin on this
useful work. And it was apparently the suggestion of the best
qualified experts, for according to a footnote the plan was based
upon the publications of the Association of German Agrarian
Societies. . . .
50   It continued in the same tone. Within a year four hundred
thousand houses for single families were to be erected, which
would at once give a million men work for a year. The undertaking
was to be partly financed by an artificial creation of credit. An
even more important point in the programme was an extensive
55   industrial autarchy. The necessary raw materials were preferably
to be obtained from friendly European Powers. Along the same
line was a demand for the abandonment of the gold standard after

the English example. The conclusion and in a sense the intellectual crown of the programme was the compulsory labour service to which all young men of a particular age were to be liable: 'there will be no exemptions for university men or other propertied persons. Every one will wield a spade.'

K. Heiden, *A History of National Socialism* (London, Methuen, 1934), pp 172–3

(d) The Nazis and agriculture

At the end the following resolution was read out and adopted unanimously:

"The thousands of Oldenburg farmers and middle-class people assembled today in the Lindenhof, together with the tens of thousands of their fellow-countrymen, who have come here in the most bitter distress to give visible expression of their despair, having listened to the speech of the National Socialist Reichstag Depty Wilhelm Kube of Berlin, declare their absolute determination not to be deceived, misled, exploited and expropriated.

"We have recognised that the distress of agriculture is inseparably bound up with the political misery of the whole German people; that parliamentarism which is corrupt through and through and a weak government are unable to overcome the German political and economic emergency.

"Let us do away with this Marxist-capitalist extortion system that has made Germany, our homeland, powerless, without honour, defenceless, and that has turned us free German farmers and the middle-class people into poor, misused slaves of the world stock exchange.

"But let us also do away with the professional federations who not only throw dust in our eyes and neutralise any vigorous action because politically they stand in the camps of the Dawes Plan. The middle class and the farmers of Oldenburg see in the German National Socialist Hitler movement the only salvation from the parliamentary morass, from the pathetic and cowardly fulfilment policy.

"Only when Germany is reborn in power, freedom and honour, led by unselfish German men who are not burdened by the contemptible policy of the last few years, only then will the German farmer stand as a free man on free soil serving the great German community as the backbone of our people.

It was noted that after the meeting several farmers approached Reichstag Deputy Kube to secure him for talks in the countryside.

Niedersachsisches Staatsarchiv 'A meeting in Oldenburg, Jan 1928' from J. Pool and S. Pool, *Who financed Hitler?* (London, Futura Publications, 1980), p 121

Questions

★   a   What effects did the Wall Street Crash have on Germany? Why did the middle classes in particular feel that they were suffering?

    b   What appeals did the Nazis make to: (i) shopkeepers; (ii) students; (iii) the unemployed?

    c   How did the Nazis appeal to the farming community (extract d)?

★   d   Why did the Nazis make great gains amongst the middle class and the farmers? Which other groups did they appeal to? Which groups did not provide much support?

★   e   Who did the Nazis blame for the economic troubles? How justified are these accusations?

(e) September 1930 – election results

When Hitler said to the Reichswehr: "With your help I could conquer," this, in March 1929, implied an extraordinary amount of self-confidence. The party, with its eight hundred thousand electors, had anything but a victorious appearance. But the number
5   of unemployed rose in 1930 to the hitherto undreamed-of figure of three millions. The economic crisis wiped out the means of livelihood. Large sections of the people began to have doubts regarding the system, but of the bourgeois parties none attacked the system so unsparingly as Hitler. The Communist agitation
10   only embraced the proletarians. Under the Government of a Social-Democratic Chancellor, Hermann Müller, Germany succumbed to the crisis. At the instigations of Groener and Schleicher – both of them Reichswehr leaders – Hindenburg withdrew confidence from Müller, the Social Democrat, and
15   summoned Dr. Brüning, the leader of the Catholic Center Party. The latter had not a majority in the Reichstag, and founded a sort of semi-dictatorship, based on the authority of the aged President; he dissolved the Reichstag and hoped that his new and energetic leadership would impress the electors and secure many votes for
20   the parties who supported him as Chancellor. The electors, however, merely saw Brüning's energy, without understanding it. The Chancellor himself remained alien to the people, a semi-dictator and not a popular figure. Who could profit by this situation? Now Hugenberg atoned for having used his whole
25   glorious apparatus merely to aggrandize his rival, Hitler. The decisive feature of the Reichstag election which took place on September 14, 1930 was, however, the participation of 4,600,000 new electors, who had never before gone to the ballot-box – a comparatively small number of them young; most of them
30   unpolitical individuals, whom, the crisis had shaken out of their previous complacency.

On the night of September 14–15, 1930 the new manager of the
Frankfurter Zeitung, Dr. Rudolf Kircher, was skeptical about the
first figures received. He was told that the Nazis were in many
35   places as strong as the Social Democrats, or even stronger.
"None the less, they will only get forty or, at most, fifty seats,"
said Kircher. "Say sixty, if you like, but that's the maximum."
One of his colleagues who had reconnoitered the country wrote
that Hitler would get at least a hundred seats. Kircher thought that
40   this was sheer imagination. But towards three in the morning he
was confronted with the staggering fact that Hitler's adherents had
in two years grown from eight hundred thousand to six and a half
million voters, and that the National Socialists with their 107
Reichstag deputies had become overnight the second strongest
45   German party.
Kircher lay back in his chair overcome. "The Germans are even
stupider than I had believed," he said.

> K. Heiden, *Hitler, A Biography* (New York, Alfred A.
> Knopf, 1936), pp 240–1

(f) Electors 1924–30

ELECTIONS	(% VOTE) NSDAP	DNVP	DVP	Centre	DDP	SPD	KPD	Others
4 May 1924	6.5	19.5	9.5	16.6	5.7	21.6	12.6	8.3
7 Dec. 1924	3.0	20.5	10.1	17.3	6.3	26.0	9.0	7.8
2 May 1928	2.6	14.2	8.7	15.2	4.8	29.8	10.6	13.7
14 Sept. 1930	18.3	7.0	4.9	14.8	3.5	24.5	13.1	14.4

> T. Childers, *The Nazi Voter* (Chapel Hill and London,
> University of North Carolina Press, 1983), pp 58 ff.

(g) Hitler's explanation

"There are only two possibilities in Germany: do not imagine that
the people will for ever go with the middle party, the party of
55   comprises: one day it will turn to those who have most consistently
foretold the coming ruin and have sought to dissociate themselves
from it. And that party is either the Left: and then God help us!
for it will lead us to complete destruction – to Bolshevism, or else
it is a party of the Right which at the last, when the people is in
60   utter despair, when it has lost all its spirit and has no longer any
faith in anything, is determined for its part ruthlessly to seize the
reins of power – that is the beginning of resistance of which I
spoke a few minutes ago. Here, too, there can be no comprise:
. . . there are only two possibilities: either victory of the Aryan or
65   annihilation of the Aryan and the victory of the Jew."

> N. Baynes (trans. and ed.), *The Speeches of Adolf Hitler
> (1922–1939)*, vol 1 (London, Oxford University Press,
> 1942), p 14

Questions

★ a What reasons does Heiden give in extract *e* for the Nazi success in the election of September 1930? What other reasons are there?

b Why might Kircher have been surprised at the magnitude of the Nazi success? Why did he claim that the German people were stupid?

c According to extract *f* which parties lost a great deal of support between 1928–30? Which parties managed to maintain their support and why do you think this was so?

★ d How good an explanation for the Nazi success is Hitler's prophecy in extract *g*?

★ e Why did people turn to the Nazis rather than to the communists in the late 1920's?

III   Manoeuvring for Power, 1930–33

Introduction

In the elections of both September 1930 and July 1932 the Nazis made sweeping gains in the Reichstag, as the economic situation got worse. Hitler's avowed politics and the sheer brutality of the S.A. Brown Shirts do not appear to have had an adverse effect. Possibly for the first time, big business began to pump money into the Nazi party seeing it as the most effective counter to the supposed communist menace.

But the election successes were still too gradual for many within the Nazi party. There were quarrels over policy and Otto Strasser resigned. Events such as the Stennes revolt showed that the S.A. were impatient for early success; there were still many who disliked the legal approach. There was also a fundamental problem with this approach. Hitler may have hoped for gains in each successive election but the Nazis never did gain an absolute majority in the Reichstag. President Hindenburg chose the chancellor and whoever filled this post increasingly tried to avoid calling the Reichstag and to rule on their own. This reduction of the power of the Reichstag may have been a useful precedent for Hitler once he came to power but for the present it meant that his electorial gains counted for little.

The chancellors had to avoid the Reichstag because they found it increasingly difficult to find supporters there. The electorate turned to extremist parties and an unholy alliance of Nazis and communists could create a majority to paralyse the Reichstag. Chancellor Brüning had to resign. Chancellor Papen attempted to form a majority government by offering the post of vice-chancellor to Hitler but he would not accept such an inferior post. When General Schleicher suggested to Hindenburg that he could gain a majority in the Reichstag and split the Nazi party by appealing to Gregor Strasser's radical wing then Papen was dismissed and Schleicher became Chancellor.

Possibly, though, Papen had stumbled on one way to weaken the Nazis. After the disastrous election results of July 1932, Papen, in desperation, called another election the following November. Nazi funds were exhausted, there was a hint of economic recovery, and for the first time the Nazis lost seats. Some historians claim that the Nazis were no longer a threat and that they were only

saved at the last moment by Papen's desire for revenge on
Schleicher and the offer, by Papen, for Hitler to be chancellor.
Papen argued later that this was natural as the Nazis were the
largest party in the Reichstag and that he did try to build in
safeguards againt a Nazi takeover: but can a democracy offer the
government to a party dedicated to destroying democracy?

1   Nazi Methods

(a) The Leipzig trial

The event of the moment in Germany is a speech made yesterday
by Hitler before the Leipzig Court before which, three officers are
appearing on charges of attempting to form National Socialist
cells within the army. One of the accused called Hitler as a witness
5   to testify 'that. the National Socialist German Workers' party
pursues its aims by legal means, that it does not aspire to upset the
Constitution or the State, that it has not called upon its members,
in 1929 also, to upset the Government'. The accused requested
Hitler to explain on broad lines the genesis of the party. . . .
10   In 1925 he decided that the movement must be brought back to
its original basis and he ordered the complete disarming of the
storm detachments, and further took steps to see that they assumed
an entirely non-military character. Raising his voice Hitler then
declared: 'We have no interest in seeing the army dissolved'. He
15   then became very worked up and after being checked by the
presiding judge he added that naturally a movement which sought
to capture the State thought first and foremost of the power of
defence. The party would, therefore, take steps to see that out of
the Reichswehr the great German citizen army would develop.
20   The presiding judge thereupon intervened with the suggestion
that reading between the lines of his statements it seemed that
Hitler was not attempting to achieve his objects by purely legal
means. In reply, Hitler claimed that he had given orders that if the
party ordinances conflicted with the law they were not to be
25   carried out. For disobedience of these orders numerous members
of the party had been expelled, including Otto Strasser, the editor
of the 'Nationaler Sozialist', who had played with the idea of
revolution. Those, he said, who spoke of a National Socialist
revolution meant a revolution of the spirit, but here Hitler
30   suddenly let himself go. 'I can assure you,' he declared, 'that if the
National Socialist movement is victorious in its fight, then there
will be a National Socialist Court of Justice, and there will be
atonement for November 1918 and heads will roll in the dust'. At
this there were loud shouts of 'Bravo!' from his supporters in the
35   galleries.

Hitler was then asked what he meant by 'German National revolution'. In reply, he stated that this was meant in a purely political sense. The National Socialists did not mean to prepare for it with illegal means. If they had two or three more elections then the National Socialist movement would have a majority in the Reichstag, and then they would prepare for a national revolution which was to raise Germany out of serfdom. 'Germany,' he declared, 'was muzzled by the peace treaties. The whole of the German legislation is to-day nothing else than an attempt to anchor the peace treaties in the German people. The National Socialists do not regard these treaties as law, but as something imposed by force. They were not prepared to burden future generations which were completely guiltless with them. When we defend ourselves against them with all possible means, then we find ourselves on the way to revolution.'

The presiding judge then interposed: 'Also with illegal means?' Hitler replied: 'I am assuming that we have won, then we shall fight against the treaties with all means, including means which, in the opinion of the world, will be regarded as illegal means.' When asked how he hoped to establish the 'Third Realm,' Hitler replied that the Constitution merely prescribed the battlefield and not the object in view. The National Socialist party would enter into existing legal institutions and would in this way make itself a decisive factor. But this it would do in a constitutional way.

Rumbold to Henderson, Berlin 26 September 1930, in E. L. Woodward and R. Butler (eds), *Documents of British Foreign Policy, 1919–39*, vol II (H.M.S.O., London, 1948), pp 514–16

(b) An attack on Otto Strasser

The situation was clarified. On the evening of July 10 when I was returning to the station through the streets of Brandenburg, just outside Berlin, with my friend, a disabled ex-soldier . . . .

We were suddenly attacked by a number of men dressed as hooligans, and I was half blinded by a handful of pepper which was thrown in my face. I wasted no time but leapt into the road and gained the opposite pavement. My attackers' aim was poor, for I was left with one eye open. I saw my friend stretched in the middle of the roadway, and our assailants were preparing to make a rush at me. I drew my revolver and shouted: 'The first man to move is dead!' I then advanced towards my injured friend, helped him up and looked back towards the pavement, holding him up with one hand and keeping our assailants covered with my revolver. They were armed only with knives and bludgeons.

Brehm was bleeding copiously and, with his wooden leg, it was not easy for us to get along. We resumed our way to the station as best we could, and I repeated my warnings to the hooligans at the top of my voice. Passers-by disappeared as if by magic. Political brawls were common at that time, and nobody wanted to be mixed up in them.

80 'I know them all, They're S.A. men,' Brehm who was a high official in that political district, whispered in my ear.

'I thought so,' I replied.

O. Strasser, *Hitler and I* (London, Jonathan Cape, 1940), p 140

Questions

a   According to extract *a* what is Hitler's attitude to relations between the army and the S.A. (storm detachments)? How satisfactory would this arrangement be for either the army or the S.A.?

b   How good is Hitler's explanation for why Otto Strasser was expelled from the Nazi party?

c   Explain the reference to November 1918 (line 33). Whose heads would roll?

d   What does Hitler mean by the phrase 'German National revolution?' (lines 36–7)? Who was he trying to appeal to in this extract? How moderate was this speech?

e   What does extract *b* show of the part violence played in German politics at this time?

f   Why might Strasser have been attacked? Do you think it would have been on Hitler's orders?

2   Democracy in Crisis

Stresemann speaking, 26 February 1929:

Let us not deceive ourselves: we are faced by a crisis in the parliamentary system which is more than a crisis of confidence. There are two causes of this crisis: first, that the parliamentary system in Germany has become a caricature of itself, and secondly,

5 the completely false view of Parliament in relation to its responsibilities towards the nation.

What is meant by the 'parliamentary system'? It means the responsibility of the Minister of the Reich to Parliament, which can, by a majority, withdraw its confidence from that Minister,

10 and compel him to resign his office. There is nowhere a condition that the Minister must be a Party man, nor that the ministerial offices shall be distributed in accordance with the strength of the groups; nor that the control shall pass from the Cabinet to the Groups. The Ministers are appointed by the President of the

15 Reich. It is clear that the President will take care that the Ministers appointed shall be such as to win the confidence of the Majority of the Reichstag.

There are movements current among the German people which emphasize the necessity of strengthening the powers of the President . . . . The President can, in conjunction with the Chancellor, undertake the formation of the Government on these lines or those, and lead the fight against a Parliament which opposes the Cabinet as formed. I am convinced that many a crisis would be at an end in a moment, if the President would utter a word in reason, and the formation of the Cabinet were removed from the negotiations of the Groups.

E. Sutton (ed.), *Gustav Stresemann – Diaries, Letters and Papers*, vol 3 (London, Macmillan, 1935), p 160

Questions

★ a Who appointed the chancellor and other ministers in the Weimar Republic? Who could bring them down?
b Why does Stresemann use the word 'Groups' (line 26)?
c Why was Stresemann arguing for a change in the political system? Would such a change be supported by the Nazi party?

3 Party Problems

(a) The Stennes Revolt

The dissensions within the National Socialist camp have now, however, introduced a new factor. The trouble began with the revolt of the 'storm detachments' under the leadership of an ex-police captain called Stennes against Dr. Goebbels, the leader of the party in Berlin. These storm detachments are said to contain '20,000 men specially trained but not politically educated'. According to the press, the storm detachments appealed direct to Hitler against the attitude adopted by Dr. Goebbels and the Berlin party committee, whom they considered too moderate and too inclined to work with the capitalists, i.e., presumably Hugenberg. Hitler, who had recently announced his willingness to work with the Constitution when it suited him, returned their manifesto to them, 'as he could not deal with rebels'. Several stormy meetings and discussions between the opposing forces in Berlin were held, at one of which, according to the 'Nationaler Sozialist' the party manager attempted to force Stennes, at the point of the revolver, to give up his demands. The news reached the local storm detachment, who foregathered and attempted to enter the building, whereupon the headquarters defence force opened fire on them, wounding several, of whom four severely. Last Sunday night twenty-five members of the disgruntled storm detachments had more success. They invaded the party headquarters, succeeded in forcing their way in and smashing everything to pieces in the large offices. . . . The headquarters guard were placed in the ignominious position of having to summon the police, who arrived in large numbers, overpowered the invaders and locked them up.

Thereupon Hitler hastened to Berlin, where he called a meeting of the members of the dissatisfied storm detachments, at which over 2,000 were said to have been present. He announced that he himself would take over the leadership of the storm detachments, and he seems to have been successful in winning them back to allegiance to the party. To do so, however, he was obliged to make concessions which in themselves are revealing. He promised to give them greater influence in the party administration after the elections. In future, too, members of the storm detachments are to pay smaller contributions than other members of the party and will have wider privileges. They will be granted compensation for legal costs and costs arising out of political conflicts, special compensation being granted to the injured or wounded.

Rumbold to Henderson, 5 September 1930, in E. L. Woodward and R. Butler (eds), *Documents of British Foreign Policy, 1919–39*, vol II (London, H.M.S.O., 1948), pp 505–6

(b) Pressures on Hitler

Hitler's thoughts at this time were wrestling with the temptation to break his own resolve to reach power by legitimate means only. He was being tempted to place himself in possession of the supreme power by a bloody revolution, a "march on Berlin". Hitler was continually being implored by his closest confederates to drop restraint and take up the revolutionary struggle. . . .

There is not the slightest doubt that an open outbreak of the National Socialist revolution was imminent at the time of the autumn elections of 1932. It would have meant the end of the party. The rising would have been ruthlessly suppressed by the Reichswehr. Over and over again in conversation this sentence cropped up: "Clear the streets for the brown battalions!" . . .

Incidentally, Hitler's followers reproached him with the charge that he had missed the most favourable moment to strike. And in truth the economic crisis began in 1932 to ease a little. The influx into the party fell off. Hitler's opponents began to draw together, and seemed well in the running. Driven to the wall, outflanked in all his chances of action, Hitler saw his plans to capture power melting away. The Reich presidential election was a heavy defeat for his party.

H. Rauschning, *Hitler Speaks* (London, Thornton Butterworth, 1939), pp 27–8

(c) Election results

	(% VOTE)							
ELECTIONS	NSDAP	DNVP	DVP	Centre	DDP	SPD	KPD	Other
31 July 1932	37.3	5.9	1.2	15.7	1.0	21.6	14.3	3.2
6 Nov. 1932	33.1	8.5	1.8	15.0	1.0	20.4	16.9	4.7

R. F. Hamilton, *Who Voted for Hitler?* (Princeton, New Jersey, Princeton University Press, 1982), p 46

(d) Nazi gloom, late 1932

Strasser, his resignation in, went into hiding. Hitler, with his own chances diving towards zero, was rushing feverishly with his aides from place to place, fighting desperately to fend off a complete Nazi collapse. One calamity followed another. The Thuringian elections of 4 December showed an ominous loss of 40 per cent from the figure of 31 July. Goebbels' diary from the beginning of December to Christmas shows the despair that gripped the Party and its leaders during those days. These are excerpts:

December 6: 'The (Nazi) situation in the Reich is catastrophic.'

December 8: 'Severe depression prevails . . . . Financial worries render all systematic work impossible . . . . The danger now exists of the whole Party's going to pieces. . . . Dr. Ley telephones that the situation in the Party is becoming more critical from hour to hour. . . . (Strasser's) letter to the Führer (resigning his offices) is dialectic pettifoggery. . . . Treason! Treason! Treason! . . . Four hours on end the Führer walks anxiously up and down the hotel room. . . . Once he stops and merely says: "If the Party should ever break up, I'll make an end of things in three minutes with a revolver.' . . .

December 10: 'The financial condition of the Berlin district is hopeless . . . . Strasser's démarche has created great alarm in the public.'

December 15: 'It is hard to hold the SA and the Party officials to a clear course. . . . If we succeed in holding the movement together we shall also succeed in saving the situation.'

December 17: 'We decide to work with all our means on the Party organization . . . and see if we cannot lift the organization up again, in spite of all.'

December 20: 'We must summon all our strength to rally the Party once more.'

December 21: 'Altercation and discord. . . . The financial crisis continues.'

December 29: 'It is possible that in a few days the Führer will have a conference with Papen. There a new chance opens.'

K. Ludecke, *I Knew Hitler* (London, Jarrolds, 1938), pp 490–1

a   What does extract *a* reveal about the political beliefs of the S.A.? Why do you think Goebbels received the blame rather than Hitler?

b   How important were the concessions made by Hitler to the rebels? Why did he treat them so leniently?

★ c   How true is the idea in extract *b* that a revolution was imminent in autumn 1932?

★ d   Why did Hitler take part in the presidential election of spring 1932? Was it a mistake to take part?

e   Look at extracts *b* and *c*. Why did Nazi support being to fall off in late 1932? Why did the DNVP begin to attract support again?

f   Why, according to extract *d*, were there problems with Gregor Strasser in late 1932? Why did he resign?

g   What problems were the Nazi party having at this time as shown in the extracts from Goebbels diary in extract *d*?

h   What is the effect of concluding the extract from Goebbels' diary with the entry for December 29?

4   Chancellors

(a) Hitler to Brüning, December 1931

You refuse as a 'statesman' to admit that if we had come in to power legally we could then break through legally. Mr. Chancellor, the fundamental thesis of democracy runs. 'All power issues from the People.' The constitution lays down the way by which a
5   conception, an idea, and therefore an organisation must gain from the people the legitimation for the realisation of its aims. But in the last resort it is the people itself which also determines its Constitution.

> N. Baynes (trans. and ed.), *The Speeches of Adolf Hitler (1922–1939)*, vol 1 (London, Oxford University Press, 1942), p 163

(b) Papen's aims

Q. What were the political aims of your cabinet? Please state this
10   briefly.
PAPEN: The central problem which occupies us was the economic one: the big economic crisis and the one and a half million unemployed young people, the six to seven million completely unemployed, and the twelve to thirteen million altogether only
15   partly employed. Attempts of my predecessors to help with purely State means proved inadequate. They were a burden on finances

and had no result. The aim of my government, therefore, was to employ private economy to solve this problem. We wanted to bring the whole production machinery into working order again. . . .

Such a programme could not have been reconciled with the parties. The political aim was, to achieve simultaneously with the reorganization of the economy, the practical co-operation of the strongest of the opposition parties, the NSDAP. That was the central problem of the German internal policy.

Q. Witness, you said a little while ago that you had no contact with Hitler before the formation of the government. When did you see Hitler for the first time and what agreements did you reach?

A. I have already said that I saw Hitler for the first time on the 9th or 10th of June. The aim of the talk was to determine under what conditions Hitler would be willing to tolerate my government. My programme contained so many points in the social field that an approval of that programme by the National Socialists was to be expected. Hitler's condition for such an approval of the government programme was the lifting of the ban on uniforms for the S.A.; that is, the political equalization of his party with the other parties.

I agreed to that at the time; all the more so as the ban of the S.A. by Brüning's government was an obvious injustice. The S.A. had been prohibited, but the uniformed formations of the Socialists and Communists, that is the "Rotfront" and the "Reichsbanner", had not been prohibited.

The result of my promise to Hitler was that Hitler bound himself to tolerate my government.

Trial of German Major War Criminals, vol 16 (H.M.S.O., London, 1946), pp 262–3

(c) Goering on the Papen government

Q. What part did you play in the appointment of Hitler as Reich Chancellor?

GOERING: If I am to explain this to the Tribunal I must first describe the situation briefly. The balance among the Parliamentary Parties had been disturbed as early as the end of 1931 or the beginning of 1932. Things were going badly in Germany and no proper enduring Parliamentary majority could actually be produced, and already at this time the Enabling Act then in force had come into play to the exclusion, in part, of the Constitution. I call to mind the Brüning Cabinet alone, which had to work to a large extent with the Enabling Act and which at the time was also greatly concerned with Article 48 of the Reich Constitution. Then there followed the Cabinet of von Papen, which also could not

put itself, on a Parliamentary basis, on a more lasting or firmer
60 basis. Herr von Papen at that time tried to make that possible and,
in order to get a Parliamentary basis, he demanded also of the
National Socialists, the strongest party at that time, that they,
together with the other Parties, establish such a basis. There was
some talk – von Papen's name had been given to the President as a
65 nominee for Reich Chancellor – that Hitler should become the
Vice-Chancellor in this Cabinet. I remember that I told Herr von
Papen at that time that Hitler could become any number of things,
but never as "Vice". Whatever he was to become, he would
naturally have to be in the highest position, and it would be
70 completely unbearable and unthinkable to place our Führer in any
sort of "Vice" position. We would then have played the role of
being governed, which was quite impossible for us; and Hitler, as
the representative of the strongest Party, would have had to cover
up these things. This we declined categorically. I do not emphasise
75 that, because Herr von Papen is in the dock with me, he knows
that we always respected him personally; but I told him then, after
this suggestion had come to naught, that we would not only
support him but would consistently fight every Cabinet which did
not give us the leading influence in the Chancellery.
80   There then came – I do not remember exactly for how many
months Herr von Papen ruled – the well-known clash between
him and me, he as Reich Chancellor, I as the President of the
Reichstag, in which it was my intention to bring his Government
to a fall, and I knew there was a motion of no confidence by the
85 Communists, in which practically everybody would participate.
. . . Thirty-two votes were for von Papen and about five hundred
were against him. The Cabinet of von Papen resigned.

> *Trial of German Major War Criminals*, vol 9 (H.M.S.O.,
> London, 1946), pp 68–9

Questions

★ a Why was Hitler speaking in favour of democracy in extract *a*?

★ b According to extract *b* why would other parties not agree with
Papen's policies? How realistic were his hopes that he would
be supported by the Nazis?

★ c Why had the S.A. been banned? How good is Papen's
explanation for the rescinding of the ban?

 d In extract *c* explain the terms 'Enabling Act' (line 56) and
'Article 48' (line 57).

★ e Why were neither Brüning nor Papen able to create a
parliamentary majority? Why would not even the moderate
parties work along with them?

★ f According to Goering why did Hitler refuse to become vice-
chancellor? What other reasons were there?

g What do these extracts reveal about the problems of the Weimar Republic at this time?

(d) A letter from Hitler to Hindenburg, 21 November 1932

Dear Herr Reichs President,

From press reports and the declaration by Secretary of State Meissner I have learned of Your Excellency's intention to ask me officially to start negotiations with other parties even before the formation of a new Presidential Government. . . .

If then, Your Excellency has called me, the leader of the National Socialist Movement, back to Berlin so that I may help to resolve this, the most difficult crisis, of our people, then I can only agree to do so with a clear conscience if the Movement and I myself are placed in the position required by the implementation of this task, and which is, in any case, due to the Movement by virtue of its strength. For the urgent need to put Germany above party will only be recognized if the strongest Movement can negotiate from the same position of strength that Your Excellency has formerly bestowed on all those wielding presidential power. Moreover this is what justice demands. For the National Socialist Movement with its 196 seats can provide any government with two-thirds of the number of delegates it needs to pass legislation.

I can make Your Excellency the firm promise that I shall provide a Presidential Cabinet formed and led by me and approved by Your Excellency with every constitutional safeguard needed in the arduous but rewarding work of resurrecting our politically and economically ruined people. I therefore have only one request to Your Excellency: to grant me at least as much authority and standing as were granted even to those who came before me and who could not contribute as much to Your Excellency's great renown and authority as I myself can.

W. Maser, *Hitler's Letters and Notes* (London, Heinemann, 1974), p 101

(e) Letter from Hindenburg to Hitler, early December 1932

You know that I prefer a Präsidial Cabinet . . . that is conducted not by a Party leader but by a man who is above Party, and that this is the kind of man in whom I should have special confidence. You have announced that you will only place your movement at the disposal of a Cabinet presided over by yourself as the Party Leader. If I agree to this plan, I must request that such a Cabinet should have a majority in the Reichstag.

K. Heiden, *Hitler, A Biography* (New York, Alfred A. Knopf, 1936), p 160

Questions

a   In extract *d* what powers was Hitler seeking as chancellor and why? Why did he refer to a 'Presidential Government' (line 5)?

b   How does Hitler try to exaggerate the Nazis' strength in the Reichstag?

c   According to extract *e* what reasons does Hindenburg give for turning down Hitler's demand to be chancellor?

★   d   Why did Hindenburg dislike Hitler? Why was this important?

(f) Schleicher replaces Papen

I therefore suggested that my Government should remain in office for the time being. We would get our economic programme working and negotiate urgently with the State Parliaments on the subject of the reform of the Constitution. There seemed no reason
5   to suppose that the newly elected Reichstag should not behave in exactly the same way as the previous one. If the Government was not going to be permitted to function, then it must do without the Reichstag altogether for a short period. Our proposed amendments to the Constitution would then be made the subject of a
10   referendum or submitted for approval to a new National Assembly. This procedure, I realized, would involve a breach of the present Constitution by the President.

The situation was so serious that I considered that the President might be justified in placing the welfare of the nation above his
15   oath to the Constitution. I told him I realized that this would be a difficult decision for a man who had always placed the value of his word above everything else, but I reminded him of the manner in which Bismarck had once found it necessary to recommend to the Prussian monarch that the Constitution should be ignored for the
20   sake of the country. Once the necessary reforms had been voted, it would be possible to return the duties of legislation to the new Parliament.

It was then Schleicher's turn. He said he had a plan which would absolve the President from taking this last drastic step. If he
25   took over the Government himself, he thought he could bring about a split in the National Socialist Party which would ensure a parliamentary majority in the present Reichstag. He then gave a detailed explanation of the differences of opinion within the Nazi movement which made it more than likely that he would be able
30   to attract the support of Gregor Strasser and about sixty Nazi members of the Reichstag. Strasser and one or two of his close supporters would be offered posts in the Government, which would be based upon the support of the Trade Unions, the Social Democrats and the bourgeois parties. This would provide a

35 majority which would make it possible to put through the
economic and social programme of the Papen Government.

I interjected here that I had grave doubts whether this plan was
feasible. It seemed to me highly unlikely that the left wing of the
Nazi Party would split off, as all the members had sworn a
40 personal oath of loyalty to Hitler. However, Schleicher's contacts
with the Nazis were much more intimate than mine, and he was
probably correct in his assumptions. In any case, the experiment
was worth making. My chief objections were of a more
fundamental nature. Ever since June 1 the President had been
45 trying to find a remedy for the collapse of parliamentary procedure.
An independent Cabinet had been formed for the purpose of
devising reforms which would ensure a more satisfactory
relationship between administration and Parliament. Schleicher's
plan would now mean that this line of action would have to be
50 abandoned. Even if Schleicher obtained his parliamentary majority,
it would not be strong enough to put through basic reforms, and
therefore would not only be a provisional solution, but a far from
satisfactory one.

F. von Papen, *Memoirs* (London, André Deutsch, 1952),
pp 216–17

(g) Schleicher's failure

PAPEN: After his efforts to split the Party and to bring about a
55 majority in the Reichstag had failed, Reich Chancellor von
Schleicher asked the Reich President to give dictatorial powers,
which meant a violation of the Constitution. Thus, he wanted the
very thing which I had proposed to the Reich President on the 1st
of December, 1932, as the only way out of the situation, a
60 proposal which the Reich President had accepted at that time but
which General von Schleicher had thwarted. . . .

Trial of German Major War Criminals, vol 9 (H.M.S.O.,
London, 1946), p 275

Questions

a   Why did Papen want to alter the constitution according to
extract *f*? In what ways did he want to change it?
b   Why did Papen assume that the new Reichstag would behave
the same as the previous one?
c   What were Schleicher's ideas? Why did he feel he could split
the Nazi party?
d   What were Papen's criticisms of Schleicher's plans?
e   Why did Schleicher fail to split the Nazi party according to
extract *g*? Why did he lose Hindenburg's support?
f   What do these extracts show about the importance of the
Nazi party in 1932?

(h) Meetings at Ribbentrop's house: Hitler and Papen

Tuesday, 10 January, 1933.
Hitler–Papen talk. Hitler will not meet Papen again until after the Lippe elections. . . .

Wednesday, 18 January.
5   In Dahlen at noon: Hitler, Röhm, Himmler, Papen. Hitler insists on being Chancellor. Papen again considers this impossible. His influence with Hindenburg was not strong enough to effect this. Hitler makes no further arrangements for talks. . . .

Saturday, 22 January.
10   Meeting at Dahlen at 10 p.m. Papen arrives alone at nine o'clock. Present – Hitler, Frick, Goering, Koerner, Meissner, young Hindenburg, Papen and Joachim. Hitler talks alone to young Hindenburg for two hours followed by Hitler–Papen talk. Papen will now press for Hitler as Chancellor, but tells Hitler that he will
15   withdraw from these negotiations forthwith if Hitler has no confidence in him.

Sunday, 23 January.
In the morning Papen saw Hindenburg who refused everything. . . .

20   Friday, 27 January.
I have never seen Hitler in such a state; I proposed to him and Goering that I should see Papen alone that evening and explain the whole situation to him. In the evening I saw Papen and convinced him eventually that the only thing that made sense was Hitler's
25   Chancellorship, and that he must do what he can to bring this about. Papen declared that the matter of Hugenberg was of secondary importance, and that he was now absolutely in favour of Hitler becoming Chancellor; this was the decisive change in Papen's attitude. Papen has become conscious of his responsibility –
30   three possibilities: a Presidential Cabinet followed by (illegible), return of Marxism under Schleicher, or Hindenburg's resignation. As opposed to these the one and only clear solution: Hitler's Chancellorship. Papen is now absolutely certain that he must achieve Hitler's Chancellorship at all costs, and that he must
35   abandon his belief that it is his duty to remain at Hindenburg's disposal. This recognition by Papen is, I believe, the turning point. Papen has an appointment with Hindenburg for Saturday at 10 a.m. . . .

Sunday, 29 January.
40   At 11 a.m. long Hitler–Papen talk. Hitler declared that on the whole everything was clear. But there would have to be general elections and an Enabling Law. Papen saw Hindenburg immediately. I lunched with Hitler at the Kaiserhof. We discussed

the elections. As Hindenburg does not want these, Hitler asked
me to tell the President that these would be the last elections. In
the afternoon Goering and I went to Papen. Papen declared that all
obstacles are removed and that Hindenburg expects Hitler to-
morrow at 11 a.m.

Monday 30 January.
Hitler appointed Chancellor.
> J. von Ribbentrop, *The Ribbentrop Memoirs* (London,
> Weidenfeld and Nicolson, 1954), pp 23–5

(i) Papen's view

Q. On the 28th of January, at noon, the Reich President instructed
you to begin negotiations for the formation of a new government.
What possibilities for the formation of a government did you
consider the political situation offered?
PAPEN: The idea of forming a parliamentary majority
government had been abandoned since the 20th of January; it was
impossible . . . . Hitler was not willing to lead or participate in
such a government.

Secondly, further support of the Schleicher Presidential Cabinet
by means of a declaration of a state of emergency and the
prorogation of the Reichstag, which was against the Constitution,
had been rejected by the Reich President on the 23rd. He had
rejected these proposals, as we know, because von Schleicher had
told him in December that a violation of the Constitution would
mean civil war and a civil war would mean chaos, "because", he
said, "I am not in a position with the army and with the police to
maintain law and order."

Thirdly, since Hitler offered to participate in a presidential
cabinet this was the only remaining possibility, and all the forces
and political parties which had supported my government in 1932
were available for this.

Q. What were the instructions which the Reich President gave
you?
A. The instructions given me by von Hindenburg were as follows:
The formation of a government under the leadership of Hitler,
with the utmost restriction of National Socialist influence, and
within the framework of the Constitution.

The safeguarding measures which I introduced at the request of
the Reich President were the following:

1. The including of a very small number of National Socialist
   ministers in the new cabinet; only three out of eleven, including
   Hitler.
2. The decisive economic departments of the cabinet to be placed
   in the hands of non-National Socialists.

85 3. Experts to be placed in the ministerial posts as far as possible.
    4. Joint reports of Reich Chancellor Hitler and Vice-Chancellor
       von Papen to Hindenburg, to avoid too extensive personal
       influence of Hitler on Hindenburg.
    5. The attempt to form a parliamentary bloc as a counter-balance
90   against the political effects of the National Socialist Party.
           Trial of German Major War Criminals, vol 9 (H.M.S.O.,
           London, 1946), pp 277–8

(j) Goering's view

In the end we, as the strongest party at that time with 232 seats,
got only the following, as far as I remember: the office of Reich
Chancellor of course; then Dr. Frick as Reich Minister of the
Interior in the Cabinet; and I next, as the third member of the
95 Reich Cabinet, with as assignment as Reich Commissar for
    Aviation – that is, of a very small subordinate division, an
    insignificant branch of a small aviation department in the Ministry
    of Transport, but no department otherwise. But then I succeeded
    in becoming, without conditions attached, Prussian Minister of
100 the Interior and thereby a political Minister of the largest German
    State, as Prussia was actually the place where the rise to internal
    power started.
        It was therefore an extraordinary difficult affair. At the last
    moment the formation of the Cabinet threatened to fail because of
105 two factors. The Führer had made the unconditional demand that
    shortly after the appointment of the new Cabinet a new Reichstag
    election should take place, knowing, correctly, that the Party
    would be greatly strengthened thereby and thus possibly could
    alone represent the majority and so be in a position to form the
110 Government platform by Parliamentary means.
           Trial of German Major War Criminals, vol 9 (H.M.S.O.,
           London, 1946), p 71

(k) The taking of power

Q. I notice that you use here, as you have used in your
interrogations by the United States, the expression "seizure of
power". That was the common expression used in your group,
was it not, to describe the coming to power of Adolf Hitler?
115 GOERING: It cannot be used in this sense. At that time it was
    completely legal, because the National Socialist Party was then the
    strongest party, and the strongest party nominated the Reich
    Chancellor and had the greatest influence. It must not be
    interpreted to mean that they usurped the power, but that they
120 had the most influential and prominent position among the parties,
    that is, by the completely legal means of election.

Q. You want to change the word "seizure"?

A. I have to change that. It is only an expression which was common usage in the Press at that time.

> *Trial of German Major War Criminals*, vol 8 (H.M.S.O., London, 1946), p 72

Questions

a Why were the Lippe elections important for the Nazi party (extract *h*)?

b What part did Papen play in Hitler becoming chancellor according to extracts *h*, *i* and *j*?

★ c Why did Hindenburg agree to Hitler becoming chancellor? How was Hitler's power to be limited?

d What demands did Hitler make in extracts *i* and *j*? Why was his power not limited, as had been intended by Papen and Hindenburg?

e In extract *k* was Goering's description correct or did the Nazis seize power?

★ f Was the Nazi party saved at the last moment, after electoral defeat, by Papen's intrigues and the offer of the chancellorship?

IV The Legal Revolution, 1933–34

Introduction

Much emphasis has been put on the fact that Hitler faced little organised opposition to his assumption of full power and that this can be explained largely by the use he made of legal methods. The latter is a moot point when one remembers that Hitler made the laws in the first place or, in extreme circumstances such as the Night of the Long Knives, was perfectly ready to pass retrospective legislation. It has been argued that Hitler was helped by a peculiarly German attitude to the law. There was less of an idea of absolute morality and absolute law: if the state made a law then it was right and was to be obeyed. Moral considerations were not important.

The lack of opposition can possibly be ascribed to other less theoretical reasons. Not only did the Nazis move quickly and, as usual, take advantage of circumstances, but there were also precedents for some actions such as the suspension of the Reichstag and interference in Prussia. The blame for starting the Reichstag fire is still a subject for discussion but in some ways it is not important; what is important is the fact that Hitler was able to take advantage of the fire to prevent the communists from taking their seats. The Enabling Act and the abolition of the trade unions were seen by some as necessary measures in desperate times. The interference in the civil service, judiciary and the dissolution of the political parties were done by turns so that it was difficult for an opposition to materialise.

How far had the Nazis taken control of the state by mid 1934? The Night of the Long Knives and the death of Hindenburg have often been seen as convenient halts on the first part of Hitler's takeover; but there was still a great deal to do.

1 Opening Moves

(a) Newspaper opinions

The Hugenberg press admits that Hitler deserves a considerable share of thanks for facilitating a solution of the crisis within 36 hours of von Schleicher's defeat. According to the 'Lokal-Anzeiger'

it must have cost him a serious effort to agree to take his seat on
the same bench as Hugenberg and von Papen. The Nazi leader has
at last, it writes, sacrificed the party idea to the general cause. The
National Socialist movement is now definitely committed to the
responsibilities of Government, and the unnatural hostility between
the two kinds of Nationalism is at an end. . . . Hitler's
abandonment of his claim to exclusive power is, the newspaper
concluded, the most significant and welcome change in the
political situation since 1918. Hitler will now have to show that he
is something more than a successful agitator. . . .

The 'Deutsche Allgemeine Zeitung' which consistently supported
the Schleicher Cabinet admits that there is some cause for
satisfaction in the reconciliation of the different sections which
compose Nationalist Germany. It goes on to say that it sees no
cause for enthusiasm in the new adventure. Hitler must have
accepted onerous conditions to have obtained what the President
refused him in November. It is curious, it writes, to find Herr
Hugenberg, who is an ardent capitalist, in the same Cabinet as
Herr Hitler, who is an ardent Socialist. It concluded rather sadly
that it is easy to appoint a Chancellor and not so easy to get rid of
him. The forces of the Left will no doubt be mobilised and
Germany will once again be torn by dissensions to the great joy
and her enemies across the frontiers.

The 'Kölnische Zeitung' and the 'National Liberal
Correspondenz' which represent the Volkspartei give free vent to
their annoyance at the complete exclusion of their party 'from the
so-called Cabinet of National Concentration'. They console
themselves with the reflection that foreign affairs, finance and
national defence are evidently withdrawn from Hitler's or
Hugenberg's control. The 'Kölnische' especially finds solace in the
thought that a strong guarantee still exists in the person of the
President of the Reich against any experiments or adventures,
whether by Hitler or Hugenberg. . . .

The Centre press maintains an attitude of cool reserve. The new
Cabinet, though admittedly a parliamentary and not a presidential
or authorative Cabinet, does not represent anything like a majority
of the German people according to 'Germania'. The newspaper
finds it odd that Hugenberg, who is the personification of
capitalism, should take his seat beside Hitler who is an equally
determined socialist. It is equally odd to find Nazi leaders
ensconced in a 'Herren Club' Cabinet in view of the vicious
campaign which the Nazi press has been conducting since last
August against von Papen and his friends. . . .

The Democratic press fails to understand why the Schleicher
Government should have been refused the right to dissolve the
Reichstag. The 'Frankfurther Zeitung' finds it monstrous that the
author of the 'Beuthen' telegram expressing sympathy with the

Potempa murderers in August last, should be solemnly installed as Chancellor of a civilised country. Hitler's personal insult to President von Hindenburg when he alluded to his advanced years and approaching demise can also not be forgotten. The Centre

55   party luckily hold the key position and their leaders are fully alive to their responsibility. There is, the paper concludes, no immediate cause for anxiety.

> Rumbold to Simon, 1 Feb. 1933 in E. L. Woodward and R. Butler (eds), *Documents of British Foreign Policy, 1919–39*, vol 4 (H.M.S.O., London, 1948), pp 402–3

(b) Limitations on the press

The new press decree of the 6th February goes far beyond anything which has yet appeared in this country. It gives the

60   Government power to suppress a newspaper once and for all, for suppression for the space of a year means economic ruin nowadays. By suppressing newspapers, proclaiming meetings, arresting speakers, and monopolising the wireless, the Government can render the task of their opponents difficult. The new decrees,

65   reversing the decision of the Supreme Court in regard to Prussia, gives the Government enormous power throughout two-thirds of the country, and one is forced to the conclusion that the President, by his two latest decrees, intends to abet the Right parties in so far as lies in his power.

> Rumbold to Simon, March 1933 in E. L. Woodward and R. Butler (eds), *Documents of British Foreign Policy, 1919–39*, vol 4 (H.M.S.O., London, 1948), p 412

(c) Filling posts

70   Q. What measures were now taken to strengthen this power after Hitler's appointment?
GOERING: It was understood by all of us that as soon as we had once come into power we must keep that power under all circumstances. We did not want power and governmental authority

75   for power's sake, but we needed power and governmental authority in order to make Germany free and great. We did not want to leave this any longer to chance, elections and Parliamentary majorities, but we wanted to carry out the task to which we considered ourselves called.

80   In order to consolidate this power now, it was necessary to reorganise the political relationships of power. That was carried out in such a manner that, shortly after the seizure of governmental authority in the Reich and in Prussia, the other States followed automatically and more or less strong National Socialist

85   Governments were formed everywhere.

Secondly, the so-called political officials, who according to the Reich Constitution could be recalled at any time – that is, could be dismissed – would naturally have to be replaced now according to custom by people from the strongest Party – as is everywhere customary.

For the further seizure of power, main political offices were now likewise filled with new appointments, as is the case in other countries when there has been a shift of power among the political Parties. Besides the Ministers there were mainly – I take Prussia as an example – the heads of provinces, the official heads of administrative districts, the police commissioners, county heads. In addition there was a certain further grade – I believe ministerial directors were considered political officials, and so also were district attorneys. This on the whole described the group of offices which were filled anew when a shift in political power took place and had previously been bargained out among the Parties having majority. It did not go so far as in other countries – there was a change of office holders, but only of the most important posts.

In spite of that we did very little in this direction at first. First of all, I requested Herr von Papen to turn over to me the position of Prussian "Minister President," since he, as he had no Party behind him, could not very well undertake this reshuffling, whereas I – that is, one of us – could do so. We agreed at once. Thereupon I filled some, a relatively small part, of the offices of the highest administrative officials of Prussian provinces with National Socialists. At the same time I generously allowed Social Democrats to remain in these posts for many weeks. . . . slowly, in the course of time, these offices, in so far as they were key presidential positions, were, of course, filled with National Socialists. . . . In the case of police commissioners, I should like to emphasise for the information of the Tribunal that the police commissioners at first had nothing to do with the Gestapo. A police commissioner in the bigger cities had the same function as a county head in the country, in part at least. These police commissioners had always been selected by the largest Parties until the seizure of power. Thus I found Social Democrats in these positions who could not, with the best of intentions, remain, as they had always been our opponents up to that date. That would have been absurd. I filled these offices of police commissioners partly with National Socialists but partly with people who had nothing to do with the Party.

Trial of German Major War Criminals, vol 7 (H.M.S.O., London, 1946), pp 72–3

(d) The official view of the Reichstag fire

'On Monday evening a fire broke out in the German Reichstag. The Reich Commissar for the Prussian Ministry of the Interior

Reich Minister Goering, on arriving at the scene of the fire immediately took charge of operations and issued the necessary orders. On receiving the news of the fire Chancellor Adolf Hitler and Vice-Chancellor Papen at once betook themselves to the scene.

'This is unquestionably the worst fire that has hitherto been experienced in Germany. The police inquiry has revealed that inflammable material had been laid throughout the entire building from the ground floor to the dome. . . .

'A policeman saw people carrying torches moving about in the dark building. He immediately opened fire upon them. One of the criminals was arrested. He was a twenty-four-year-old mason named van der Lubbe, from Leiden in Holland, and was found to be in possession of a properly-visaed Dutch passport. He stated that he was a member of the Dutch Communist Party.

'The central portion of the Reichstag had been completely gutted and the chamber in which the Reichstag held its meetings has been destroyed. The damage runs into millions. This act of incendiarism is the greatest terrorist achievement of German Bolshevism. In the hundreds of tons of pamphlets found by the police in the Karl Liebknecht House were instructions for carrying out a Communist terror after the Bolshevist pattern.

'According to these instructions government buildings, castles, museums, and vitally important factories were to be set on fire. Instructions were also found ordering that women and children, and wherever possible the wives and children of policemen, were to be used as cover by the Communists, in cases of rioting and street fighting. The discovery of this material prevented the Communists from systematically carrying out their revolution. Nevertheless the burning of the Reichstag was intended to serve as the signal for bloodshed and civil war. Raids on business houses and shops had been ordered for Tuesday at four in the afternoon. . . . This terror was to signalize the commencement of civil war.

28 February 1933 Prussian Press Bureau release, quoted in K. Heiden, *A History of National Socialism* (London, Methuen, 1934), pp 220–1

Questions

a What attitude does the Hugenberg press take towards Hitler in extract *a*?

★ b Explain the reference to the 'Potempa murderers' (line 51).

c Why did most of the newspapers feel no real cause to worry at Hitler becoming chancellor? Why did they think he would not become too powerful?

d Explain why these newspapers put different interpretations on Hitler's policies.

e   Why was the Prussian decree important in extract *b*?
f   According to Goering in extract *c* how did the Nazis strengthen their position in Germany in the first few months of power? How did he defend this method?
g   How did the Nazis take advantage of the Reichstag fire according to extract *d*? Why was there so much stress on the communist menace?
★ h   How harsh was the Emergency Decree? What effects did it have and why was it not rejected by the other parties?

2   The Enabling Act

(a) March 1933 election results

The General Election on March 5, if not the overwhelming Nazi success that subsequent plebiscites have been, nevertheless gave Hitler and his Nationalist allies a 52 per cent majority in the Reichstag. With 288 seats, representing seventeen and a quarter
5   million votes in the country, the Nazis themselves made up 44 per cent of the new House. They had the support of 52 Nationalist and Stahlhelm members, who still followed their respective leaders – Hugenberg and Seldte, both, for the present, colleagues of Hitler's in the new Ministry

> G. Ward Price, *I Know these Dictators* (London, Harrap, 1937), p 110

(b) Hitler's introduction to the act

0   "Yet it is all the more necessary that the National Government should be given that sovereign position which, at such a time, is the only one suited to prevent a different development. The Government will only make use of these powers in so far as they are essential for carrying out the vitally necessary measures.
5   Neither the existence of the Reichstag nor that of the Reichsrat are menaced. The position and rights of the President of the Reich remain unaffected. It will always be the foremost task of the Government to act in harmony with his aims. The separate existence of the federal States will not be done away with. The
20   rights of the Churches will not be diminished, and their relationship to the State will not be modified. The number of cases in which an internal necessity exists for having recourse to such a law is in itself a limited one. All the more, however, the Government insist upon the passing of the law. They prefer a clear decision in any
25   case."

> N. Baynes (trans. and ed.), *The Speeches of Adolf Hitler (1922–1939)*, vol 1 (London, Oxford University Press, 1942), p 426

(c) A summary of the Enabling Act

On 24th March 1933, only 535 out of the regular 747 deputies of
the Reichstag were present. The absence of some was unexcused;
they were in protective custody in concentration camps. Subject
to the full weight of the Nazi pressure and terror, the Reichstag
30   passed an enabling act known as the "Law for the Protection of
the People and State", with a vote of 441 in favour. This law
marks the real seizure of political control by the conspirators.
Article 1 provided: that the Reich laws can be enacted by the
Reich Cabinet. Article 2 provided: the National Laws enacted by
35   the Reich Cabinet may deviate from the Constitution. Article 3
provided: National Laws enacted by the Reich Cabinet are
prepared by the Chancellor and published in the Reichsgesetzblatt.
Article 4 provided: Treaties of the Reich with foreign states,
which concern matters of national legislation, do not require the
40   consent of the parties participating in legislation. The Reich
Cabinet is empowered to issue the necessary provisions for the
execution of these treaties.

Thus the Nazis acquired full political control, completely
unrestrained by any provision of the Weimar Constitution.

Prosecutor's speech at *Trial of German Major War Criminals*,
vol I (H.M.S.O., London, 1946), p 109

Questions

a   Explain the references in extract *a* to: (i) Reichstag (line 4);
(ii) Stahlhelm (line 7).
b   What limitations and assurances did Hitler give concerning the
Enabling Act according to extract *b*?
c   Why were so many of the deputies missing from the Reichstag
according to extract *c*?
★ d   The Enabling Act needed a two-thirds majority. How did
Hitler achieve this majority? Why did relatively few deputies
oppose the act?
★ e   How important was the act for the Nazis?
f   In what ways does extract *c* use emotive language in an
attempt to put the Nazis in a bad light?

3   Opposition

(a) The Civil Service Act

The chief preoccupation of the new régime has been to press
forward with the greatest energy the creation of uniformity
throughout every department of German life; this is called
'Gleichschaltung' a term taken from the electrical industry. . . .

Although on paper there are four other political parties in Germany besides the National Socialists, the latter are in complete command of the situation and dominate everything from the Cabinet down to the family; this is no exaggeration, because the utterance of critical remarks about National Socialism in private conversation may easily result in imprisonment.

Strange as it may seem, probably the proportion of National Socialists in the Cabinet is less than in any other body in the country, but this does not in the least affect the supremacy of the party.

In the course of the imposition of uniformity, the German Federal States have almost ceased to exist as separate national entities, and it is proposed to manifest this fact outwardly by the abolition of the designation 'Bavarian', 'Saxon', etc., in passports and other official documents and the substitution of the term 'German'. The officialdom of the States, no less than that of the Reich, has been purged of Jews and Marxists, the process embracing clerical employees, and labourers in State employ. The same method has been applied to the municipalities, provincial districts and to the social organisations. A legal basis for this cleansing operation has been created by the passage of a number of laws, the most important of which is the Civil Service Act of the 7th April, which has been taken as a model for similar regulations and actions throughout the country regarding the professions and trade and industry. The important provisions of this law may, therefore, be briefly given. They are as follows:-

a) Officials appointed since 9th November, 1918, who have not had the education appropriate to their post or are otherwise not suited to it, are to be dismissed.

b) Officials who are not of Aryan descent are to be retired, unless they were officials on or before the 1st August, 1914, or fought at the front for Germany or one of her allies, or lost their father or sons in the war.

c) Officials whose political activities hitherto do not offer a guarantee that they will at all times support the national state without reserve, can be dismissed, but shall receive, if they have more than ten years' service, three-quarters of their pension.

In order to bring the nation as far as possible into conformity with this purified civil service, similar principles have been applied by the authorities or by the party to all professions, trades, acts, sports and education.

Rumbold to Simon, 26 April 1933 in E. L. Woodward and R. Butler (eds), *Documents of British Foreign Policy, 1919–39,* vol 5 (H.M.S.O., London, 1948), pp 864–5

(b) Hitler's May Day speech, 1934

When on 2 May last year we began the destruction of the party-system in Germany by laying hands upon the Trade Unions, that was done not in order to rob any Germans of representative
50 institutions serving a useful purpose, but to free the German people from those organs the greatest abuse of which was that they were forced to encourage abuses in order to prove the necessity for their own existence. By so acting we have rescued the German people from an incalculable amount of internal strife
55 and discord which benefited no one save those who were directly interested in maintaining that discord, but always wrought fatal mischief upon the whole people.

N. Baynes (trans. and ed.), *The Speeches of Adolf Hitler (1922–1939)*, vol 1 (London, Oxford University Press, 1942), p 892

Questions

a Who was the Civil Service Act directed against according to extract *a*? How precise was it? Why were non–Aryans involved in World War I exempt from the act?

b How important was it to reduce the powers of the Federal States?

★ c Why did other political parties cease to exist during this period?

d In extract *b* how did Hitler explain the dissolution of the Trade Unions? Why were the unions unable to defend themselves effectively?

★ e Which groups did the Nazis not control at this time?

4 Party Opposition

(a) A complaint from the American ambassador

October 11. Wednesday. The Dutch Minister called, ... The subject of atrocities came up and I told him of the shameful case of a Woolworth store man in Dusseldorf being attacked on the streets there last Sunday in a most disgraceful way. The last such
5 case occurred on September 1. After ample time and promises over the telephone by the police authorities, I had gone to Von Neurath, Foreign Minister, and had an hour or nearly that with him. He regretted every one of the eight or ten cases that were listed to him and promised everything one could ask, but said,
10 "The S.A. men are so uncontrollable that I am afraid we cannot stop them," repeating, "I will do all possible." On Thursday, October 5, I had sent a request to the Foreign Office urging a

report on what officials had done. No reply came, which I think
means that the police have taken no measures against the guilty
men.

> W. E. Dodd Jr and M. Dodd (eds), *Ambassador Dodd's Diary
> 1933–38* (London, Gollancz, 1941), p 57

(b) Röhms' complaints

In his reproaches against the Reichswehr he was unjust and
embittered. He resented the arrogant reserve of the Reichswehr
officers. . . .

"Adolf is a swine," he swore. "He will give us all away. He
only associates with the reactionaries now. His old friends aren't
good enough for him. Getting matey with the East Prussian
generals. They're his cronies now."

He was jealous and hurt.

"Adolf is turning into a gentleman. He's got himself a tail-coat
now!" he mocked.

He drank a glass of water and grew calmer.

"Adolf knows exactly what I want. I've told him often enough.
Not a second edition of the old imperial army. Are we
revolutionaries or aren't we? Allons, enfants de la patrie! If we are,
then something new must arise out of our elan, like the mass
armies of the French Revolution. If we're not, then we'll go to the
dogs. We've got to produce something new, don't you see? A
new discipline. A new principle of organisation. The generals are
a lot of old fogeys. They never had a new idea."

> H. Rauschning, *Hitler Speaks* (London, Thornton
> Butterworth, 1939), pp 154–5

(c) Hitler on the S.A.

I asked whether this plan included the general arming of the S.A.
and S.S., and whether it had been definitely discarded.

'This plan is discarded,' Hitler replied. 'Enthusiasm and
willingness are not enough. The arming and equipment of a great
army is a serious and difficult problem. My S.A. men are
disappointed. They have reproached me in terms which I have had
to reject as unjustified. What did they imagine, I asked them?
Could I recommend that Germany should have two mutually
independent armies?'

'. . . were the party members to give voluntary service and be
bound to the army for a specially long period? Or were all the
members of the S.A. to belong to a special military elite, or was I
to use them as a sort of people's militia?'

'. . . No, I must say the arguments of my S.A. men have not convinced me. I have every intention of keeping to my agreement and my obligations to Hindenburg and the army.'

H. Rauschning, *Hitler Speaks* (London, Thornton Butterworth, 1939), p 133

(d) Hitler on Gregor Strasser

Hitler frowned. "Strasser would do better to attend to the smooth functioning of the political organization, and stop trying to formulate Nazi policy. He's extended himself too far, and I'll have to dock his tail pretty soon. If the masses want socialism, let them expect it – and vote for it. Strasser is committing the Party to more than we shall be able to give."

K. Ludecke, *I Knew Hitler* (London, Jarrolds, 1938), p 427

(e) A warning from Rudolf Hess

The attitude of the National Socialist Party to the question of the department stores remains unaltered in principle. A solution will be found for it when the right time comes in the sense of the National Socialist programme. In view of the general economic situation the Party leaders feel they are not at present called upon to proceed towards the destruction of department stores and similar undertakings. Hence members of the National Socialist Party are forbidden until further notice to engage in any action against department stores or similar undertakings.

July 7 announcement quoted in K. Heiden, *Hitler, A Biography* (New York, Alfred A. Knopf, 1936), p 130

(f) A warning from Hermann Goering

It does not lie with us to say if a second revolution is necessary. The first revolution was ordered by the Leader and finished by him. If the Leader wishes a second revolution, we stand to-morrow, if he wants us, in the streets. If he wishes no further action we will suppress every one who wants to make a second revolution against the wishes of the Leader.

That is the idea which everyone must take as his own idea, for about things touching the machinery of state as a whole in its fundamentals, only the Leader has the right to say the final word. I also want to accentuate the following: As much as we would never dare to venture without the Leader to undertake a revolutionary act, so I wish on the other hand, to leave no doubt in the minds of any that we watch keenly and observe all. Further, we will not tolerate that all these things for which we struggled in this revolution, shall be destroyed behind our backs by lower orders or by the purposely misconstruing of legislation. From this perhaps may spring sabotage and it will lie with you to stop such sabotage at the right time.

> Speech 18 June 1934 from *The Political Testament of Hermann Goering* (London, John Long, 1938), p 102

(g) A complaint from Papen

There appears to be endless talk of a second wave which will complete the revolution. Anyone who irresponsibly toys with such ideas should not deceive himself about the fact that a second wave can easily be followed by a third, that he who threatens the guillotine is the first to come under the knife. Nor is it clear in what direction this second wave is meant to lead. It is true that there is much talk about future socialisation. Have we experienced an anti-Marxist revolution in order to carry out the programme of Marxism? For any attempt to solve the social question by collectivising property is Marxism. . . .

No Nation that would survive before history can afford a permanent uprising from below. At some stage the movement must come to an end; at some point there must emerge a firm social structure held together by a legal system secure against pressure and by a State power that is unchallenged. A ceaseless dynamic creates nothing. . . .

In the long run, therefore, the State cannot tolerate any dualism, and the success of the German revolution and the future of our nation will depend on the discovery of a satisfactory solution for the dualism between Party and State.

> Quoted in J. Noakes and G. Pridham (eds), *Nazism 1919–1945*, vol 1 (Exeter, University of Exeter, 1983), p 121

Questions

a In extract *a* why was it significant that Woolworth was involved in the attack?

b What attitude did Dodd take in this statement? Why might the Nazis have been worried by American objections?

c Von Neurath was a traditional politician. What do his replies suggest of the relationship between the administration and the Nazi party?

d According to Rauschning in extract *b* what complaints did Röhm have concerning Hitler? How is this account dramatised?

★ e How good an explanation of Hitler's objections to the S.A. is extract *c*? Why was it important at this time for Hitler to keep his 'obligations to Hindenburg and the army' (line 50)?

f What were Strasser's ideas according to extracts *d*, *e* and *f*?

Why did Goering have to issue warnings to other members of the Nazi party?

★ g How important was von Papen's warning according to extract g? Was his a correct assessment of the views of Röhm and Strasser?

(h) Hitler's explanation for the Night of the Long Knives

Without ever informing me and when at first I never dreamt of any such action, the Chief of Staff Röhm, through the agency of an utterly corrupt swindler — a certain Herr von A—, entered into relations with General Schleicher. General Schleicher was the man
5 who gave external expression to the secret wish of the Chief of Staff, Röhm. He it was who defined the latter's views in concrete form and maintained that:

1. The present régime in Germany cannot be supported.
2. Above all the army and all national associations must be united
10 in a single band.
3. The only man who could be considered for such a position was the Chief of Staff, Röhm.
4. Herr von Papen must be removed and he himself would be ready to take the position of Vice-Chancellor, and that in
15 addition further important changes must be made in the Cabinet of the Reich. . . .

However, in the course of the 29th of June I received such threatening intelligence . . . .

At 1 o'clock in the night I received from Berlin and Munich
20 two urgent messages concerning alarm summonses. Firstly that for Berlin an alarm muster had been ordered . . . for 4 o'clock in the afternoon, that for the transport of the regular shock-formations the requisition of lorries had been ordered, and that this requisition was now proceeding, and that promptly at 5
25 o'clock action was to begin with a surprise attack: the Government building was to be occupied. . . .

In these circumstances I could make but one decision. If disaster was to be prevented at all, action must be taken with lightning speed. Only a ruthless and bloody intervention might still perhaps
30 stifle the spread of the revolt. . . .

"If anyone reproaches me and asks why I did not resort to the regular courts of justice for conviction of the offenders, then all that I can say to him is this: in this hour I was responsible for the fate of the German people, and thereby I became the supreme
35 Justiciar of the German people!"

Speech to the Reichstag, 13 July 1934 in N. Baynes (trans. and ed.), *The Speeches of Adolf Hitler, 1922–1939*, vol 1 (London, Oxford University Press, 1942), pp 311, 319–20

(i) The army's approval

The Army's role is clearly determined; it must serve the National Socialist State, which it affirms with the deepest conviction. Equally it must support those leaders who have given it back its noblest right to be not only the bearer of arms, but also the
40   bearer, recognized by State and people, of their unlimited confidence. . . . In the closest harmony with the entire nation . . . the Army stands, loyal and disciplined, behind the rulers of the State, behind the President, Field Marshal von Hindenburg, its Supreme Commander, and behind the leader of the Reich, Adolf
45   Hitler, who came from its ranks and remains one of ours.

General von Blomberg, Minister of Defence, quoted in A. Bullock, *Hitler, A Study in Tyranny* (Harmondsworth, Penguin, 1962), p 301

(j) Hindenburg's testament, 11 May 1934

My Chancellor Adolf Hitler and his movement have made a decisive step towards the great goal of bringing the German people together to an inner unity above all differences of rank and class. I know that much remains to be done and I wish with all
50   my heart that, behind the act of national resurgence and national coalescence, there shold be an act of conciliation comprising the entire German Fatherland.

. . . I say farewell to my German people in the firm hope that that for which I longed in the year 1919 and which by a slow
55   maturing process led to 30 January 1933, will mature to the complete fulfilment and consummation of the historic mission of our people.

In this firm faith in the future of the Fatherland I am content to close my eyes!

Quoted in W. Coole and M. Potter (eds), *Thus Spake Germany* (London, Routledge, 1941), p 116

(k) Law concerning the head of the Reich, August 1 1934

60   I The office of the Reich President is hereby united with that of the Chancellor. The authority hitherto exercised by the Reich President hence passes to the Führer and Chancellor, Adolf Hitler. He shall appoint his deputy.

II This law shall become effective from the moment of the death
65   of President von Hindenburg.

Quoted in L. L. Snyder (ed.), *Documents of German History*, (New Brunswick, Rutgers University Press, 1958), p 424

Questions

a Who did Hitler blame for the supposed plot in extract *h*? Who did he claim it was directed against?

b Why did Hitler have to defend himself? What defence did he make? Why was Blomberg's statement important according to extract *i*?

★ d Röhm, Schleicher and Gregor Strasser were killed amongst others. Why were these three killed? Why are exact numbers of those executed hard to put together?

★ e Why did the 'Night of the Long Knives' take place?

★ f What was Hindenburg's attitude towards the Nazis according to extracts *j* and *k*? How important was extract *k* for Hitler? Why was it somewhat premature? What part did Hindenburg play in the government in the last year of his life?

V Domestic Policy: Support

Introduction

The nature of Hitler's rule continues to puzzle historians. The traditional view is of the all-powerful Führer, in total control of both party and country. A variant on this is the idea that Hitler was passionately interested in some areas, foreign policy in particular, and was quite content to leave the day-to-day running of other departments to his underlings. But a third interpretation sees Hitler as a very weak individual, continually duped by various of his top party men who only fed him the information that they wanted to give him.

Possibly by design, there is equal confusion over the relations not only between leader and party but also between party and state. Even in power, Hitler disliked being specific. In broad terms, National Socialism believed in a hierarchy of leader, party leaders, ordinary party members, the German people. Why should the people support such a system? For one thing, the supposed classless system in Germany meant that in theory anyone, regardless of birth, could get to the top. Secondly, by a purely cynical view, Hitler seems to have believed that he could keep the people happy by giving them what they wanted: a buoyant economy, an organised life revolving around Nazi institutions and free trips on the Rhine were seen as an easy way to stay in power. This is a point hard to prove.

The economy was obviously of great importance to the Nazis and once again there is argument over many areas. Was Hitler interested in the economy at all? Did the Nazis plan the economy, attempt to bring in socialist policies or leave everything to big business? The situation is further complicated by Hitler's deliberate attempts to portray the German economy as geared to total war. German arms production was impressive, but Hitler could exaggerate for effect. Many at the time saw the German economic boom as too good to be true. Where was the finance coming from? Self-sufficiency and rearmament were very expensive. Doubts were cast on the validity of the Four-Year Plans. Many have suggested that by the late 1930's Hitler was running out of money rapidly: so did World War II begin because force was the only way to gain further resources?

1 Leader and Party

(a) An insider's view

In the eyes of the people Hitler was the Leader who watched over the nation day and night. This was hardly so. But Hitler's lax scheduling could be regarded as a life style characteristic of the artistic temperament. According to my observations, he often allowed a problem to mature during the weeks when he seemed entirely taken up with trivial matters. Then, after the "sudden insight" came, he would spend a few days of intensive work giving final shape to his solution. No doubt he also used his dinner and supper guests as sounding boards, trying out new ideas, approaching these ideas in a succession of different ways, tinkering with them before an uncritical audience, and thus perfecting them. Once he had come to a decision, he relapsed again into his idleness. . . .

After 1933 there quickly formed various rival factions that held divergent views, spied on each other, and held each other in contempt. A mixture of scorn and dislike became the prevailing mood within the party. Each new dignitary rapidly gathered a circle of intimates around him. Thus Himmler associated almost exclusively with his SS following, from whom he could count on unqualified respect. Goering also had his band of uncritical admirers, consisting partly of his closest associates and adjutants. Goebbels felt at ease in the company of literary and movie people. Hess occupied himself with problems of homeopathic medicine, loved chamber music, and had screwy but interesting acquaintances.

As an intellectual Goebbels looked down on the crude philistines of the leading group in Munich, who for their part made fun of the conceited academic's literary ambitions. Goering considered neither the Munich philistines nor Goebbels sufficiently aristocratic for him, and therefore, avoided all social relations with them; whereas Himmler, filled with the elitist missionary zeal of the SS (which for a time expressed itself in a bias for the sons of princes and counts), felt far superior to all the others. Hitler, too, had his retinue, which went everywhere with him. Its membership, consisting of chauffeurs, the photographer, his pilot, and secretaries, remained always the same.

A. Speer, *Inside the Third Reich* (London, Weidenfeld and Nicolson, 1970), pp 195, 83

(b) Hitler's speech at Nuremburg, 1935

The function of the State is the continuance of the administration, as it has in the course of history arisen and developed, of the State organs within the framework of and by means of the laws.

The function of the Party is:

40 1. The building up of its own internal organisation so as to create a stable, self-renewing, permanent cell of National Socialist teaching.
    2. The education of the entire people in the meaning of the conception of this idea.
45 3. The introduction of those who have been so trained into the State to serve either as leaders or as followers. . . .

At present the ferments of the old party-state are still working, and thus during this transitional period it may happen that the Party finds itself compelled to intervene by way of warning and, if
50 necessary, of correction when the leaders of the State are contravening National Socialist principles. But this correction in future can only be effected through the agency of the competent State-institutions and authorities which are already occupied by National Socialists. The final goal must be, through winning over
55 all Germans to National Socialism, that in the future only National Socialists shall be admitted to any posts in the whole organisation alike of the people and of the State.

> N. Baynes (trans. and ed.), *The Speeches of Adolf Hitler (1922–1939)*, vol 1 (London, Oxford University Press, 1942), p 244

(c) Goering's view

The party had the duty to set high aims for the national work of the people – the aims that were born of the national socialist point
60 of view. It has to bring public life into tune with these aims and to keep it there. It has, and that is the more important task, to train the leaders of the future and to place them at the disposal of the people when called upon to do so. Lastly, it has to recruit the people and to bring them up as national socialist compatriots. In
65 the more important matters, steps have been already taken – in fact, directly after we came to power. You have only to remember that leading posts in the state are filled by leading national socialists.

> *The Political Testament of Hermann Goering* (London, John Long, 1938), p 159

Questions

a According to extract *a* what was Speer's opinion of Hitler's style of leadership? Why did he stress the disunity in the leading party members?

★ b 'The antagonisms of power were only resolved in the key position of the omnipotent Führer.' (K. D. Bracher). Did Hitler exercise complete control over the party or did he merely preside over a situation of 'organised chaos'?

★ *c* To what extent did leading Nazis such as Goering and Himmler build up their own areas of power?

★ *d* Compare the views expressed in extracts *b* and *c* on the role of the party. What was the role of the state? To what extent was the party merely an elite group controlling society and to what extent was it expected to infiltrate and influence all aspects of the community?

2 State and People

(a) Hitler's speech to the Reichstag, 23 March 1933

"The splitting up of the nation into groups with irreconcilable views, systematically brought about by the false doctrines of Marxism, means the destruction of the basis of a possible communal life. The disintegration attacks all the foundations of
5 social order. The completely irreconcilable views of different individuals with regard to the terms State, society, religion, morals, family and economy give rise to differences that lead to internecine war. Starting from the liberalism of the last century, this development is bound by natural laws to end in communistic
10 chaos." . . .

"It is only the creation of a real national community, rising above the interests and differences of rank and class, that can permanently remove the source of nourishment of these aberrations of the human mind."

N. Baynes, (trans. and ed.), *The Speeches of Adolf Hitler (1922–1939)*, vol 1 (London, Oxford University Press, 1942)

(b) Hitler on mass meetings

15 Mass assemblies are also necessary for the reason that, in attending them, the individual who felt himself formerly only on the point of joining the new movement, now begins to feel isolated and in fear of being left alone as he acquires for the first time the picture of a great community which has a strengthening and encouraging
20 effect on most people. Brigaded in a company or battalion, surrounded by his companions, he will march with a lighter heart to the attack than if he had to march alone. In the crowd he feels himself in some way thus sheltered, though in reality there are a thousand arguments against such a feeling.

A. Hitler, *Mein Kampf* (London, Hurst and Blackett, 1939), p 397

(c) The divided society

The ordinary party member was being taught that grand policy
was much too complex for him to judge it. Consequently, one felt
one was being represented, never called upon to take personal
responsibility. The whole structure of the system was aimed at
preventing conflicts of conscience from even arising. The result
was the total sterility of all conversations and discussions among
these like-minded persons. It was boring for people to confirm
one another in their uniform opinions.

Worse still was the restrictions of responsibility to one's own
field. That was explicitly demanded. Everyone kept to his own
group – of architects, physicians, jurists, technicians, soldiers or
farmers. The professional organizations to which everyone had to
belong were called chambers (Physicians' Chamber, Art Chamber),
and this term aptly described the way people were immured in
isolated, closed-off areas of life. The longer Hitler's system lasted,
the more people's minds moved within such isolated chambers. If
this arrangement had gone on for a number of generations, it
alone would have arrived at a kind of caste society. The disparity
between this and the Volksgemeinschaft (community of the
people) proclaimed in 1933 always astonished me. For this had the
effect of stamping out the promised integration, or at any rate of
greatly hindering it. What eventually developed was a society of
totally isolated individuals. For although it may sound strange
today, for us it was no empty slogan that "the Führer proposes
and disposes" for all.

> A. Speer, *Inside the Third Reich* (London, Weidenfeld and
> Nicolson, 1970), p 67

(d) A united society?

The national socialism of our Weltanschauung came therefore at
the right time. Our movement seized hold of the cowardly
marxism and took from it the meaning of socialism. It also
deprived the cowardly middle class parties of their nationalism
and, throwing both into the cauldron of our Weltanschauung,
there emerged crystal clear the synthesis: German National
Socialism! That was the foundation of the rebuilding of our
nation. That is why this revolution was a national socialistic one.
The idea grew out of the nation itself – and, because it grew out of
the nation, led by the unknown corporal of the Great War,
therefore this idea was also chosen to put an end to the dissension
among the people and once more to unite them into one unit. The
outer frame of the Reich was weak – it was only in existence on
paper; inside there was the people, torn apart and bleeding from a
thousand wounds; inside there was opposition – of all parties,

65 professions, classes, confessions, and occupations. Our leader, Adolf Hitler, realised that the Third Reich could only be saved and rebuilt if one could put inside this outer frame a united people. And that was the work of our movement during the past fourteen years – to make out of a people of divergent interests, 70 religions, classes and occupations – a new and united German people.

> *The Political Testament of Hermann Goering* (London, John Long, 1938), pp 36–7

(e) The classless society

I do not ask you all where you come from!

I have on my staff, officers specially selected from among the common soldiers, and have learned to respect them as real men. 75 One may come from the poorest of conditions; from the most insignificant family, yet in truth he carries in his rucksack the marshal's baton. How much he may make out of himself in life depends entirely on him alone. To-day, nothing is a drawback. Conceited appearances of accident may have been wiped away, 80 the individual man is tested and stands, as a result, on his own value. And with that all weaknesses fall away which once contributed to the making of cleavages within the officers' corps itself. Therefore I desire, and command of you, that you take the people's community, created by the Leader, as an example, and 85 that you become part of it – and that you count more valuable the poorest compatriot, than perhaps the richest and most prominent foreigner. Only when all of us think and feel like that will we become an unconquerable people's community.

> *The Political Testament of Hermann Goering* (London, John Long, 1938), p 187

(f) The role of education

The attainment of high intellectual standards will certainly continue 90 to be urged upon the young people, but they will be taught at the same time that their achievements must be of benefit to the national community to which they belong. As a consequence of the demand thus clearly formulated by the Nuremberg Laws, Jewish teachers and Jewish pupils have had to quit German 95 schools, and schools of their own have been provided by and for them as far as possible. In this way, the natural race instincts of German boys and girls are preserved; and the young people are made aware of their duty to maintain their racial purity and to bequeath it to succeeding generations. As the mere teaching of 100 these principles is not enough, it is constantly supplemented, in the National Socialist State, by opportunities for what may be called "community life". By this term we mean school journeys, school camps, school "houses" in rural neighbourhoods, and similar applications of the corporate principle to the life of schools and scholars.

J. von Ribbentrop quoted in B. Rust, *Germany Speaks* (London, Butterworth, 1938), p 110

Questions

a What were Hitler's views on the united, national community according to extracts *a* and *b*? Why, according to Hitler, was society usually divided?

b Explain Speer's alternative views on society under Hitler in extract *c*. How does this extract compare with that in extract *a* (page 70) on the power of Hitler?

c What is meant by 'The state is a community of living beings' according to extract *d*? What was the folk society and why was it stressed by the Nazi party?

★ *d* In extract *e* why does Goering refer to 'cleavages within the officers' corps itself' (lines 82–3)? Who would this extract appeal to? In what ways is this extract representative of Nazi beliefs?

e How was education intended to fit in with the Nazi ideas on the community of all Germans according to extract *f*?

★ *f* To what extent did the Nazis in Germany create a classless and united society?

3 Party and People

(a) Functionaries of the NSDAP and its affiliates, 1934

Organisation	*Number*
PO (Political Organisation: administration)	373.000
NSBO (National Socialist Organisation of Factory Cells: part of DAF)	120.000
NS-Hago (Kampfbund and middle class: small businesses)	57.000
NSKVO (Veterans Welfare Organisation)	25.300
Amt fur Beamte (Staff of NSBB)	34.000
NS Womens League	53.000
a.A (Office for Agriculture)	20.000
N.S. Teachers Organisation	12.700
N.S. Association of Physicians	1.500
NS Lawyers Association	1.600
NS Welfare Organisation	68.000
Organisation for communal affairs	3.600
Party Courts	2.500

Organisation	Number
Propaganda Offices	14.000
Press Offices	7.400
Hitler Youth	205.000
Reich Labour Service	18.500
TOTAL	1017.000

20

Volkischer Beobachter, 25 Feb 1934, quoted in D. Orlow, *The History of the Nazi Party*, vol 2 (Newton Abbot, David and Charles, 1971), p 92

(b) Hitler on the workers

'I am a socialist, and a very different kind of socialist from your rich friend Reventlow. I was once an ordinary working-man. I would not allow my chauffeur to eat worse than I eat myself. But your kind of socialism is nothing but Marxism. The mass of the
25 working classes want nothing but bread and games. They will never understand the meaning of an ideal, and we cannot hope to win them over to one.'

O. Strasser, *Hitler and I* (London, Jonathan Cape, 1940) p 124

(c) Hitler's address to the Reichstag, 20 February 1938

"The following are the achievements for the welfare of the working population."
30 "The wage arrangements before the advent of the National Socialist regime may be summed up as follows: 13,000 wage schedules, bargaining between groups out for their own interests, hard-and-fast agreements, levelling of working conditions, wages under the standard log, struggles for power, strikes, and lock-
35 outs, general dissatisfaction."

"After five years of National Socialist constructive work: 7,000 wage schedules, clearly defined legal relations, no hard-and-fast agreements, but minimum basic rates, wage scales according to performance, no class-war with strikes and lock-outs, no wages
40 under log standard, effective protection of all social interests, social settlement through the German Labour Front, social peace all round."

"Holidays before the National Socialist regime:
"Holidays mostly at the worker's own expense, no legal claim,
45 long period of waiting before the first holiday granted, insufficient holiday period, at the most 5 days."

"After five years of National Socialist constructive work: Each working individual has a claim to holiday with pay, minimum and not maximum holiday fixed, grading of holidays according to

length of service in firm, age, number of years employed and
difficulty of work: a short period of waiting, as a rule only 6
months, before the first holiday is granted, increased holiday
period up to 18 days for young person, holidays also for seasonal
workers, healthy recreation by means of cheap 'Kraft durch
Freude' tours."
  "Wage-policy before the National Socialist regime:
  "Wage equals price for article 'work', schematic maximum
wages, wages influenced by unemployment, wages below log
standard, piece-work under pressure, no stability of income, loss
of earnings on public holidays."
  "After five years of National Socialist constructive work:
Assurance of the right to work, assurance of minimum income,
increase of wages with the increase of production, relation of
wages to performance, stability of income, sound and honest
piece-work conditions, preferential treatment for large families,
payment for public holidays."
  N. Baynes (trans. and ed.), *The Speeches of Adolf Hitler
  (1922–1939)*, vol 1 (London, Oxford University Press,
  1942), pp 962–3.

Questions

a What does the table in extract *a* show of the Nazis' involvement
   in society? Which aspects of society did they concentrate on in
   particular?
b What does extract *b* show concerning Hitler's attitude towards
   the workers? What did he mean by the term Socialist (as in
   National Socialist)? How did this differ from Marxism?
★ c According to extract *c* how had the Nazis improved life for the
   workers? How far was this improvement merely concerned
   with welfare? What rights did the workers lose under Nazi
   rule?
★ d From the information given in these extracts and other sources
   is it possible to assess how far the general public actively
   worked with and supported the Nazi party?

4 The Economy

(a) Agriculture

Agriculture is officially under the Ministry over which Dr.
Hugenberg presides, but the National Socialists are obtaining a
firm hold on it by installing their representatives in agricultural
chambers throughout the country. In his programmatic speech on
the 21st March the Chancellor attached very great importance to
the maintenance and support of agriculture, and he said quite

frankly that the fulfilment of this object would involve sacrifices on the part of the remainder of the people who are consumers of agricultural produce. In agriculture, as in industry, the tendency
10 will be to help the farmers and the settlers rather than merely to preserve the large estates, as was the policy of earlier Governments.

An act has been passed to assist agricultural tenants; it deals with the conditions under which they may give or be given notice. A strong bid is also being made to strengthen the influence of the
15 farmers in the Ministries, particularly the Prussian Ministry of Agriculture.

There has been an important combination of the existing agricultural associations, that is the Landbund, the National Socialist Farmers' Federation and the Federation of Christian
20 Farmers' Unions, who have come together in the new Association of Agricultural Leaders.

> Rumbold to Simon in E. L. Woodward and R. Butler (eds),
> *Documents of British Foreign Policy 1919–39*, vol IV
> (H.M.S.O., London, 1948), p 866

Questions

a Why did Hugenberg have control over agriculture at first? What problems were the farmers facing?

★ b Why did the Nazis attach such great importance to agriculture? In what ways did agriculture fit their views on the folk society and race?

c Why is there a stress on helping agricultural tenants? Which 'earlier governments' had attempted to preserve the large estates and why?

★ d How did the Nazis help agriculture? Was it given special attention or was it subordinated to the Nazi economy as a whole?

e In what ways was the forming of an 'Association of Agricultural Leaders' a typical Nazi move?

(b) Hitler's speech to the Reichstag, 21 May 1935

What happens is that in so far as we are deprived of foreign markets for our exports we are forced to restrict our imports. To that extent, so that German productive labour may not stagnate, we must either employ a complicated process for the production
5 of raw materials that we lack internally or else we must use substitutes. This task can be undertaken only by means of a planned economic system. . . .

What we have achieved in two and a half years in the way of a planned provision of labour, a planned regulation of the market, a
10 planned control of prices and wages, was considered a few years

ago to be absolutely impossible. We only succeeded because behind these apparently dead economic measures we had the living energies of the whole nation. We had, however, first to create a number of technical and psychological conditions before we could carry out this purpose. In order to guarantee the functioning of the national economy it was necessary first of all to put a stop to the everlasting oscillations of wages and prices. It was further necessary to remove the conditions giving rise to interference which did not spring from higher national economic necessities, i.e. to destroy the class organizations of both camps which lived on the politics of wages and prices. The destruction of the trade unions, both of employers and employees, which were based on the class struggle demanded an analogous removal of the political parties which were maintained by these groups of interest, which interest in return supported them. Here arose the necessity for a new constructive and vital constitution and a new organization of the Reich and State.

> N. Baynes (trans. and ed.), *The Speeches of Adolf Hitler (1922–1939)*, vol 1 (London, Oxford University Press, 1942), pp 910–11

(c) Private enterprise

You ask whether private economic interest will have to be eliminated. Certainly not. I have never said anything of the kind, nor have I deputed any of my subordinates to say so. That would be as mad as an attempt to abolish social intercouse by decree. The instinct to earn and the instinct to possess cannot be eliminated. Natural instincts remain. We should be the last to deny that. But the problem is how to adjust and satisfy these natural instincts. The proper limits to private property and private enterprise must be drawn through the state and general public according to their vital needs. . . . The needs of a state, varying according to time and circumstances, are the sole determining factor.

> H. Rauschning, *Hitler Speaks* (London, Thornton Butterworth, 1939), p 134

(d) Economic expansion

"That the silent motor-works would not only spring into life but would be enlarged on an unheard of scale."

"That the production of motor-cars would rise from 45,000 in the year of 1932 to some quarter of a million."

"That in four years the deficits of our States and cities would be wiped out."

"That the Reich would gain from taxation an annual increase of nearly five milliards."

"That the German Imperial Railway would at length recover, and that its trains would be the quickest in the world."

"That to the German Reich would be given roads such that since the beginnings of human civilization they have never had their match for size and beauty: and that of the first 7,000 kilometres which were planned already after not quite four years 1,000 kilometres would be in use and over 4,000 kilometres would be in course of construction."

"That enormous new settlements with hundreds of thousands of houses would come into being, while in ancient cities of the Reich mighty new buildings would arise which may be said to be the greatest in the world."

"That hundreds upon hundreds of gigantic bridges would be thrown over gorges and valleys."

N. Baynes (trans. and ed.), *The Speeches of Adolf Hitler (1922–1939)*, vol 1 (London, Oxford University Press, 1942), pp 652–3

(e) Schacht and the New Plan

The obstacles which were placed in the way of Germany's exports everywhere progressively limited her opportunities to buy goods abroad. We needed foreign foodstuffs and we could pay for them only with industrial goods. Before we could pay for them only with industrial goods. Before we could manufacture these industrial goods we needed raw materials which were unobtainable in Germany and had to be got from abroad. As foreign countries did not buy sufficient goods from us we were unable to obtain sufficient foreign exchange to pay for the purchases we desired to make. The problem seemed particularly insoluble.

I began my search for a solution from the very simple principle that Germany must refrain from buying more than she could pay for, in order to prevent an accumulation of foreign debt which would make a proper trade balance still more difficult to establish in the future. If a country cannot pay for everything it would like to buy, then for the time being at least it must buy only the things it most urgently needs, and it must buy them wherever the terms of trade are most favourable to it. Now 'the most favourable' is not always equivalent to 'the cheapest'. In this respect other countries had taught us a thing of two. The system of important quotas had closed markets to German goods even when they were the best and cheapest obtainable on those markets. The corollary was not difficult to see. If a country has insufficient foreign exchange to permit it to buy what it needs anywhere and everywhere, then the question of cheapness ceases to be of interest, and the main question becomes whether it is possible to obtain the desired goods anywhere at all, even at high prices. Might it not

therefore be possible to find countries which would be willing to
sell their goods not against payment in their own currency, but
90 against some other consideration? This other consideration in our
case could only be German goods. Thus I had to look around for
agricultural and raw material producing countries which would be
willing to take German goods in exchange for the foodstuffs and
raw materials they produced. Bilateral commercial agreements
95 with such countries were the solution. . . .

The New Plan had born fruit. The passivity of our foreign trade
balance had given way to an export surplus. The foreign exchange
situation had been improved, both foodstuffs and raw materials
were being imported in adequate quantities and unemployment
00 had been completely abolished. All that was now necessary to
keep our economic situation stable was for us to go on working
calmly along these lines. However, that did not suit either Hitler's
mentality or his intentions. Everything had to be bigger and to be
done quicker. . . .
05 Germany's rearmament had to fit into the framework of the
New Plan – or break it.

Even during the course of 1935 I began to exert pressure on the
Armed Forces to keep the speed and extent of their rearmament
within reasonable bounds.

H. Schacht, *Account Settled* (London, Weidenfeld and
Nicolson, 1949), pp 80–1, 89–90

(f) Goering on economics

10 We do not recognise the sanctity of some of these so-called
economic laws. It must be pointed out that trade and industry are
servants of the people, while capital also has a role to play as the
servant of economy.

Naturally, the economic experts and economic leaders will
15 always, from their own standpoint, point out the need for raw
materials as economic necessities and their expert judgment will
always be the foundation on which the statesmen will base their
final decisions. But beyond this, for his decision on measures, the
statesman has also to take into consideration the foreign political,
120 domestic political and psychological problems as factors, the
knowledge of which, as a whole, is not as a rule generally known
to the economists. In order to awaken the understanding of the
whole nation and of every economist to his problems, the
statesmen will again and again appeal to the whole economic and
125 political workers for a correct attitude to economy – to the factory
owners as well as to the workmen.

The Political Testament of Hermann Goering (London, John
Long, 1938), p 211

(g) A critic on Goering and the Four Year Plans

Goering set out with all the folly and incompetence of the amateur to carry out the programme of economic self-sufficiency, or autarky, envisaged in the Four Year Plan. He exploited the plenary
130 powers Hitler had given him as chief of the Four Year Plan operations in order to extend his own influence over economic policy, which he did not find difficult, since he was now, of course, in a position to place really large contracts. Under the banner of this 'Four Year Plan', decree followed decree. On
135 December 17th, 1936, Goering informed a meeting of big industrialists that it was no longer a question of producing economically, but simply of producing. And as far as getting hold of foreign exchange was concerned it was quite immaterial whether the provisions of the law were complied with or not,
140 provided only that foreign exchange was brought in somehow. Whoever succeeded in obtaining foreign exchange would go scot free even if he had broken the law. Only those who broke the law without succeeding in obtaining foreign exchange would be prosecuted. In other words Goering proclaimed the dissolution of
145 all economic order and the introduction of jungle morality. It was incumbent on me to denounce this economic nonsense, and to oppose this irresponsible and wanton flouting of the law, as openly as possible.

I gave Goering my public answer in a speech at a celebration
150 organized by the Reich's Chamber of Economics in honour of my sixtieth birthday. The audience was more or less the same as that which had listened to Goering's December speech, so that my allusions were generally understood. . . . referring to the economic aspect of the question I declared: "Assuming that technical means
155 remain the same, then there is no getting round the fact that if I proceed to work iron ore of 30 per cent ferrous content where I previously worked iron ore of 60 per cent ferrous content, then I shall need double the amount of labour power, double the amount of transportation, double the blast-furnace capacity, etc., to
160 produce the same result with 30 per cent ore that I previously produced with 60 per cent ore. That is to say, gentlemen, that I must cut production at some other point if I am suddenly to concentrate my energies on this." And further: "If anyone says: 'The important thing is to produce, not to produce profitably,' I
165 say to you that if you produce uneconomically you will waste the substance of the German people. . . . If I sow a hundred-weight of grain on a certain area of land and harvest only three-quarters of a hundredweight, then that is the most utter economic nonsense imaginable."
170 Goering's policy of recklessly exploiting Germany's economic substance necessarily brought me into more and more acute

conflict with him, and on his part he exploited his powers, with Hitler and the party behind him, to counter my activity as Minister of Economics to an ever-increasing extent.

> H. Schacht, *Account Settled* (London, Weidenfeld and Nicolson, 1949), pp 98–9

(h) An outsider's view

Another dangerous aspect of the situation was Germany's increasing financial and economic difficulties. The strain, both mental and material, under which the German people had been working since 1933 was immense, and required an increasingly violent psychological stimulus to keep it working. It was estimated in 1938 that sixty per cent, or more of the sum of her efforts in human beings, labour, and materials were destined for war. No people, even though disciplined and hard-working as are the Germans, would put up indefinitely with guns instead of butter, or endure an economic policy based solely on wehrwirtschaft – namely, the control of the whole of a nation's economic output in the interests of military preparedness. There was always the question, therefore, whether Hitler would not feel obliged to seek to conquer by force the markets which Germany had lost by over-concentration on armaments, or, in other words, be compelled to follow the road of further adventure, either in order to forestall economic collapse or as the result of it.

Economic disaster spelt unpopularity for Hitler and for Nazism, and to many thinking Germans the real problem was whether Hitler could change his economic policy and revert to normalcy without another internal revolution. . . . I was always disinclined to accept the over-simplified theory that Hitler would necessarily be obliged to seek further adventure in order to avoid economic collapse. I had too high a respect for the capacity of German organisation to regard such a theory as the whole truth.

> N. Henderson, *Failure of a Mission* (London, Hodder and Stoughton, 1940), pp 198–9

Questions

a   In extract *b* what did Hitler mean by the idea of a 'planned economic system' (line 7)?

★   b   To what extent did Hitler argue in extract *c* against planning in the economy? In what ways does this extract fit in with Nazi beliefs? How far does it contradict the ideas put forward in extract *b*?

★   c   Did Hitler move from a policy of opposing big business before he came to power to one of support for it once he was in office? Why have Marxist historians often stressed the idea that Hitler was controlled or influenced by big business?

d   Which projects does Hitler mention in extract *d*? Why did the Nazis concentrate on large projects and to what extent were these projects based on military needs?

e   What was the New Plan and how did it work according to extract *e*? With which countries did Germany make bilateral commercial agreements?

f   Extract *e* comes from a book written by Schacht after the war. Why did he emphasise the fact that the Plan would not work if rearmament went ahead too rapidly?

g   Some historians have suggested that the Nazis had little real understanding of economics and that Hitler merely demanded that the economy find more and more money for rearmament. How far do extracts *f* and *g* support this view?

h   According to Schacht, how were the Four Year Plans intended to achieve economic self-sufficiency? How important was this aim? How successful was this policy?

i   What did the Schacht-Goering clash show of the relationship between state experts and party officials?

★   j   What fears did Henderson say that some people had about the Nazi economy in extract *h*? To what extent was the German economy geared to war? Was it true that the Nazis had chosen 'guns not butter'?

VI *Domestic Policy: Opposition*

Introduction

National Socialism always stressed many hatreds, particularly of other political beliefs and other races. Sadly, hatred is also a good way of uniting any group or people by giving them something to unite against. People appear to have been arrested for a wide range of offences and organised opposition seems to have been of little effect. Political parties and religious groups were fatally fragmented and forced underground. The military would appear the only major opposition available yet it is difficult to assess their potential at the time.

Oppression also existed for those whose only crime was to exist: the senile, the mentally ill and, in particular, the Jews. Even in the case of the Jews, there are differing interpretations. Some historians argue that Hitler's anti-semitism was just an early vote winner, to be played down once in power and with the eyes of the world upon him. The extermination of the Jews had yet to be agreed upon; the concentration camps that did exist by the mid 1930's were vicious and there were deaths but, as yet, not on an organised, industrial scale.

The attempts by the Nazis to show the concentration camps as better than they were was but one aspect of the Nazi organisation of oppression. The Secret State Police, and even the courts, used a deliberate vague policy to upset the people in which one might disappear for no reason and never be heard of again. When each street or block of flats might have its own Nazi informer, then it was obviously dangerous to voice a contrary opinion.

How much coercion was needed is hard to gauge. Did the German people support the Nazis? After World War II it was usually suggested that Hitler and the Nazis had managed to fool most of the people for most of the time and had imposed themselves on the population. The alternative explanation, that Hitler and the Nazis were genuinely accepted by a large proportion of the German people, means taking a more jaundiced view of human nature: and naturally it would be hard today for a historian now to find people in Germany who would admit to having once supported the Nazis.

1 The System of Repression

(a) The government's view

Compatriots! my measures will not be vitiated by any legal doubts. My measures will not be weakened by any bureaucracy. Here I have not to exercise righteousness; here I have only to destroy and to clear. Nothing else. This fight, compatriots, will
5 be a fight against chaos and such a fight I do not lead with ordinary police means. That a 'state of citizens' may have done. Certainly I will also use the full powers of the state and the police to their utmost measure, my dear communists, in order than you do not draw wrong conclusions, but the fight to the death, in
10 which I will 'put my fist in your necks', I will lead with those down there, my brownshirts! I will make it clear to the people that they have to defend themselves. I will make it clear to them that all strength has to be mobilised, and therefore I declare with full purpose: "In future, gentlemen, only those can enter the state
15 who come from the national strength and not those who crowd around and lie."

I am not disturbed when certain 'critics' get excited about these measures and cry for more 'justice'. I measure with two measures. I would not be just if I did not send the communists to hell at last.
20 Too long have they lounged about in easy chairs and lived on our money – it is high time they went! Fourteen years long they have oppressed this national Germany, and for fourteen years not even a porter in a ministry was allowed to be a national socialist. That was 'justice' for you! For fourteen years they have suppressed it.
25 No. He who acknowledges the state now, him the state will recognise – but he who tries to destroy the state, him the state will destroy.

> The Political Testament of Hermann Goering (London, John Long, 1938), pp 26–7

(b) Judicial support

It is important in the Führer principle that a statement by the Führer promulgated in a special form, for instance a proclamation
30 at a Party Rally, or in the Reichstag, or his judgement of 30 June, 1934, is to be regarded as a source of law and has to be carried out by the judges. . . .

As the sources of interpretation, the judges have at their disposal the Party Programme, Mein Kampf and speeches by the Führer.

> Justice Rothenburger, 4 October 1935, quoted in W. Coole and M. Potter (eds), Thus Spake Germany (London, Routledge, 1941), p 112

(c) The law and the state

35 Q. Were the political police posts of the German States occupied by Party members in 1933?
A. No, those posts were occupied by former police. Only a few officials were newly taken on at that time.
Q. Were the leading officials members of the Party?
40 A. That varied in the various States. There were even officials who had formerly held quite different views and belonged to other parties.
Q. Can you give an example of this?
A. There are several well-known examples. It is well known that
45 Herr Diehls, the Chief of the Prussian Secret State Police, had formerly held other political opinions.
The closest colleagues of Himmler and Heydrich from Munich, who were taken with him to the Office of the Secret State Police in Berlin – such as Mueller, who later was head of (Dept.) Amt
50 IV; Huber, Fresch, Beck – they were formerly adherents of the Bavarian People's Party. . . .
Q. Why, then, did these officials continue in the police service under National Socialist rule?
A. For a German official it was a matter of course to keep on
55 serving the State, even though the Government changed – as long as he was in a position to do so.
Q. Were these officials removed and later on replaced by National Socialists?
A. No, these gentlemen had mostly a very successful career and
60 obtained good posts.
> Hermann Goering at *Trial of German Major War Criminals*, vol 20 (H.M.S.O., London, 1946), p 143

(d) The police

Q. How did the additional recruiting of personnel for the political police take place in the years that followed?
A. Officials from the German police agencies were transferred to the offices of the political police. In the course of time new
65 candidates were also enlisted and were trained to become officials according to the general rules which were applicable for the appointment and the training of officials.
Q. Were people taken on from the Party, from the SS and the SA?
70 A. Only in a relatively small way, as service in these police agencies brought in very little in wages and therefore was not very much sought after.
Q. Did the officials volunteer to enter the political police?
A. The officials were transferred from one office to another.

75 Q. Did the officials have to comply with these transfers?
A. Yes, according to civil service laws they were bound to do so.
Q. What would have been the consequence of a refusal?
A. Disciplinary action, with the result that they would have been dismissed from office, with the loss of their acquired rights; for
80 instance, their right to a pension.
Q. Do you know of any such refusal?
A. No, I have not heard of any.
Q. Was the political police completely separated from the general administrative set-up of the State?
85 A. No, on all levels there was a close liaison with the general interior administration.

> Hermann Goering at *Trial of German Major War Criminals*, vol 20 (H.M.S.O., London, 1946), p 143

(e) The secret state police

The Secret State Police is an official machine on the lines of the Criminal Police, whose special task is the prosecution of crimes and offences against the State, above all the prosecution of high
90 treason and treason. The task of the Secret State Police is to detect these crimes and offences, to ascertain the perpetrators and to bring them to judicial punishment. The number of criminal proceedings continually pending in the People's Court on account of high treasonable actions and of treason is the result of this
95 work. The next most important field of operations for the Secret State Police is the preventive combating of all dangers threatening the State and the leadership of the State. As, since the National Socialist Revolution, all open struggle and all open opposition to the State and to the leadership of the State is forbidden, a Secret
100 State Police as a preventative instrument in the struggle against all dangers threatening the State is indissolubly bound up with the National Socialist Leader State. The opponents of National Socialism were not removed by the prohibition of their organisations and their newspapers, but have withdrawn to other
105 forms of struggle against the State. Therefore, the National Socialist State has to trace out, to watch over and to render harmless the underground opponents fighting against it in illegal organisations, in camouflaged associations, in the coalitions of well-meaning fellow Germans and even in the organisations of
110 Party and State before they have succeeded in actually executing an action directed against the interest of the State. This task of fighting with all means the secret enemies of the State will be spared no Leader State, because powers hostile to the State from their foreign headquarters, always make use of some persons in
115 such a State and employ them in underground activity against the State.

The preventative activity of the Secret State Police consists primarily in the thorough observation of all enemies of the State in the Reich Territory. As the Secret State Police cannot carry out, in addition to its primary executive tasks, this observation of the enemies of the State, to the extent necessary, there marches by its side, to supplement it, the Security Service of the Reichsfuhrer of the SS, set up by his deputy as the Political Intelligence Service of the movement, which puts a large part of the forces of the movement mobilised by it into the service of the security of the State.

The Secret State Police takes the necessary police preventive measures against the enemies of the State on the basis of the results of the observation. The most effective preventive measure is, without doubt, the withdrawal of freedom, which is covered in the form of protective custody, if it is to be feared that the free activity of the persons in question might endanger the security of the State in any way. The employment of protective custody is so organised by directions of the Reich and Prussian Minister of the Interior and by a special arrest procedure of the Secret State Police, that, as far as the preventive fight against the enemies of the State permits, continuous guarantees against the mis-use of the protective custody are also provided.

Volkischer Beobachter, 27 Jan 1936, quoted in *Trial of German Major War Criminals*, vol 3 (H.M.S.O., London, 1946), p 188

(f) Local party officials

Under Paragraph 1, "The sense and purpose of card indexing households," it is stated that the purpose is a basis for statistical inquiries and, combined with the entries on the back of the card index of households, for the political judgment of the members of a household.

Then a few lines farther on, the information contained on them must enable the Ortsgruppenleiter to give at any moment a judgment of the household member concerned which is sufficient in all respects.

Then, my Lord, under Paragraph 5, "The Blockleiter must be in possession of lists which contain the same printed text as the household card index, and which are to be provided with the necessary entries by the Blockleiter: family status, Party Membership, membership of an organization, affiliated body, etc."

On the next page, the second paragraph in No. 10 sets out the information which is to be obtained. Half-way down the paragraph it says: "It is thus to be recorded since when the Volksicher Beobachter was subscribed to, whether the family already possessed a swastika flag before the 1935 flag law, and what wireless apparatus is available in the household. It is easy to obtain

this data from a conversation by Blockleiter with the German
160 concerned."

The next paragraph deals with the political judgment of the
inhabitants. . . .

Then in the last paragraph, No. 14 on the next page, it describes
how this information can be obtained. "It is prohibited on principle
165 to give Germans and Party members lists or index cards to fill in
themselves. Owing to their frequent visits to the individual
households, the Blockleiter have sufficient opportunity to obtain
the required data for the index by means of conversations with the
Germans. . . .

170 My Lord, the next document, still on the same subject, is D-
902, which will become Exhibit GB 542. A report sent to the
Erfurt Branch Office of the Security Service, marked confiden-
tial. . . .

"After thorough and most careful examination in the area of the
175 Ortsgruppe of Melchendorf and in the closest co-operation with
the Ortsgruppenleiter, we have come to the following conclusion:

The following persons will, with 100 per cent probability, vote
'No' at the forthcoming plebiscite."

Then, after setting out the names, it gives what they call
180 "explanations" in the case of each.

"Explanation:
1. Wilhem Messing (taken into protective custody in 1933 because
   of illegal activity for the Communist party . . .) and so on.
2. Walter Messing (also taken into protective custody in 1933 for
185   slandering the SA)."

> *Trial of German Major War Criminals*, vol 20 (H.M.S.O.,
> London, 1946), pp 129, 131

Questions

a What was Goering's attitude towards legal processes according
   to extract *a*? Who did he claim was the main threat to Germany
   and why was this so?

b Explain the reference in extract *b* to 'the judgement of 30 June,
   1934' (lines 30–1). Why was this incident important in relation to
   the Nazis' attitude towards the law?

c Which sources did the judges claim for the basis of laws? What
   would have been the more usual sources?

d Many countries accept that the law and the judiciary are largely
   separate from the state. What does extract *c* show of the
   attitude of some Germans towards judicial/state relations? Why
   did so few officials object to the Nazis?

e What was Goering's opinion on police/party relations according
   to extract *d*? What does this account suggest concerning the
   ordinary German's attitude towards the Nazis?

f According to extract *e* what different purposes had: (i) the Criminal Police; (ii) Secret State Police; (iii) Security Service of the S.S.?

g What was the main role of the Secret State Police? Why, according to extract *e*, were they Nazi rather than just state police?

h What was the role of the 'Blockleiter' according to extract *f*? What impression does this extract give of the Nazis' control over the people?

★ i In what ways does this extract give a false view of Nazi police methods and their opponents?

2 The System in Action

(a) An individual attack

I now asked about this brother-in-law, and learned that during the Republic he had been an outspoken Social Democrat. When President von Hindenburg appointed Herr Hitler Chancellor on 30th January 1933, this man issued a pamphlet warning citizens
5 against the encroaching dangers of dictatorship. After the Reichstag fire on February 27th he had stated, without reserve, his opinion that the National-Socialists had done this themselves to unloose a wave of terror and ride to power on it.

He had worked hard to oppose them in the March elections,
10 and issued a pamphlet against the proclamation of the anti-Jewish boycott of April 1933. He had tried to form a league of men and women organized to fight the "Law of April 7th" when published, because he felt that its "reform of the organization of the Reich" simply meant the handing of government over to complete Nazi
15 control. He had issued a pamphlet telling Catholics that the Concordat signed between Hitler and the Vatican on July 8th would be betrayed by Hitler as soon as he had made what use he could of the Catholics.

On July 16th, not quite six months after Hitler became
20 Chancellor, a law was published forbidding all parties except the National-Socialist Party. Shortly afterwards this man went for a walk one evening and did not return. At Christmas the wife shot their five-year-old son and herself "while of unsound mind". She had that morning received a package – a cigar box – marked with
25 a swastika and the word "traitor" before her husband's name. It contained ashes.

N. Waln, *Reaching for the Stars* (London, The Cresset Press, 1940), pp 79–80

(b) The concentration camps

One day 180 new prisoners arrived. The beatings lasted from about six in the evening until about one o'clock in the morning. The screams of the beaten men were heard through the whole
30 camp. At half-past one the camp doctor arrived. When he (himself an S.A. man) saw the condition of the beaten men, he boiled over with indignation. 'You swine,' he roared at the tormentors, 'You're not human beings, you're beasts. . . .' I may as well tell you that our camp counted as a model camp and was therefore shown to
35 the representatives of the foreign Press. . . . One day the meals were remarkably good. That meant, we knew, a visit, and next day it occurred. . . . The guards took care that we were well dressed, and then the journalists appeared – accompanied of course by S.A. men and conducted by the Commandant. It had been
40 arranged that we should be found sitting at games – chess, cards etc. . . . The journalists asked us whether we were satisfied. In consideration of the fact that S.A. men, with rubber truncheons, stood behind us, we said, "Yes." Whether the food was good? Again, in consideration, etc., . . . and so on. In short, the
45 journalists have received the best impression. . . .

One Brown Shirt used to amuse himself by kicking over the urine pail. . . . A man might be made to gather a pailful of small stones from outside the wire entanglement, by pushing his arms between the barbed wires. The blood was, of course, soon running
50 down his arms. . . . One o'clock one Sunday night a half-drunken S.A. man came into the dormitory. "Someone has been smoking here," he said. "By your leave," said the prisoner in charge, "there has been no smoking. "What, you want to be impudent?" In two minutes all the dormitory had to be fully dressed for inspection.
55 They had then to exercise in the snow. Back to the room. In two minutes all had to be in bed. Again up and dress. Exercise in the snow. Back again. Undress again. Up again. So it went on fifteen times that night.

H. Picton, *Nazis and Germans* (London, Allen and Unwin, 1940), pp 103–4.

Questions

a Explain the references in extract *a* to: (i) 'the anti-Jewish boycott of April 1933 (lines 10–11): (ii) 'the Law of April 7th' (line 12); (iii) the Concordat of July 8th (line 16); (iv) the Law of July 16th (lines 19–20).

b What does this extract show of Nazi methods? Would this incident have been centrally organised or merely a local move?

c What impression of the concentration camp system is given in extract *b*? What types of person were put into such camps?

d Why were journalists from other countries invited to these camps?

e What impression were both these accounts trying to give of Nazi Germany and towards whom were they directed? To what extent do they suggest an organised policy of oppression?

3 The Church

(a) Church and State

The teaching of religion, of the denominations, is under the protection of the state. But the Reich is neither Catholic nor Protestant, but German. . . . The attitude of the individual to the denominations will not be regulated by the state. The state . . .
5   leaves it to the individual to regulate his attitude to Religion and Weltanschauung for himself. . . . The state has no objection if the individual finds that his Weltanschauung has become his Religion, nor on the other hand, if he adheres to the traditional denominations and attempts to find a balance between the two. But the state will
10 not tolerate one thing: namely that the principle of the teaching should lie in the Church dogmas rather than in the philosophy of life of the community.

> German newspaper quoted in E. Buller, *Darkness over Germany* (London, Longmans, Green and Co., 1943), pp 76–7

(b) The Evangelical Church

The Hitler Government soon saw that it would both be convenient for them and in accordance with their general plans for the reorganisation and unification of the country if they could forward
15 the movement for unity in the Evangelical Church. Although so many National Socialists were Church people that a body called 'German Christians' was formed within the party to forward party aims inside the Church, the Government were careful to leave the work of reorganisation to the Churches themselves, and
20 it eventually became possible to proceed with the choice of a single head for the various branches of the Evangelical Church.

> Rumbold to Simon, 8 June 1933 in E. L. Woodward and R. Butler (eds), *Documents of British Foreign Policy 1919–39*, vol 5 (H.M.S.O., London, 1948), p 896

(c) Beliefs of the Evangelical Church

6. We demand a revision of the political clauses of our Church treaty and a fight against unreligious and unpatriotic Marxism

25   and its Christian-Socialist train-bearers of all shades. We miss
        in the present treaty the venturing confidence in God and in the
        mission of the Church. The way to the Kingdom of Heaven is
        through struggles, the cross and sacrifice, not through a false
        peace. . . .
30   8. We see in a soundly conceived Home Mission a living
        Christianity of action which, however, from our point of view
        has its roots, not in mere compassion, but in obedience to the
        will of God and in gratitude for Christ's death on the cross.
        Mere compassion is 'charity' and leads to presumption, paired
35   with a bad conscience, and effeminates a nation. We know
        something about Christian obligation and charity toward the
        helpless, but we also demand the protection of the nation from
        the unfit and the inferior. The Home Mission must not in any
        case contribute to the degeneration of our nation. In addition,
40   it must keep aloof from economic adventures and must not
        become a shopkeeper.
     9. We see a great danger in our nationality in the Jewish Mission.
        It promises to allow foreign blood into our nation. We object
        to the Jewish mission in Germany so long as the Jews have the
45   citizenship and so long as there is the danger of racial mixture
        and bastardization. The Holy Scriptures tell us also something
        about holy wrath and self-denying love. Marriages between
        Jews and Germans particularly must be prohibited.
            From the ten points of 'German Christians' for an Evangelical
            Reich Church, quoted in J. Conway, *The Nazi Persecution
            of the Churches* (London, Weidenfeld and Nicolson, 1968),
            p 341

(d) Catholic objections

        The struggle against the Church did, in fact, become ever more
50   bitter; there was the dissolution of Catholic organisations; the
        gradual suppression of the flourishing Catholic schools, both
        public and private; the enforced weaning of youth from family
        and Church; the pressure brought to bear on the conscience of
        citizens, and especially of civil servants; the systematic defamation,
55   by means of a clever, closely organised propaganda, of the
        Church, the clergy, the faithful, the Church's institutions, teachings
        and history; the closing, dissolution, confiscation of religious
        houses and other ecclesiastical institutions; the complete suppression
        of the Catholic Press and publishing houses. . . .
60   In these critical years, joining the alert vigilance of a pastor to
        the long-suffering patience of a father, our great predecessor, Pius
        XI, fulfilled his mission as Supreme Pontiff with intrepid courage.
            But when, after he had tried all means of persuasion in vain, he
        saw himself clearly faced with deliberate violations of a solemn

pact, with a religious persecution masked or open but always
rigorously organised, he proclaimed to the world on Passion
Sunday, 1937, in his Encyclical 'Mit brennender Sorge' that
National-Socialism really was: the arrogant apostasy from Jesus
Christ, the denial of His doctrine and of His work of redemption,
the cult of violence, the idolatry of race and blood, the overthrow
of human liberty and dignity. . . .

> Papal Encyclical, 1937, quoted in *Trial of German Major
> War Criminals*, vol 3 (H.M.S.O., London, 1946), p 50

Questions

★   *a*   Explain the term in extract *a* 'Weltanschauung' (line 6).
    b   What view was taken here of the rights of religion under the
       Nazis?
★   *c*   What was the Evengelical Church according to extracts *b* and *c*?
       In what ways was it a National Socialist Church?
★   *d*   What areas of life was the Roman Catholic Church involved in
       according to extract *d*? To what extent did it oppose Hitler
       during this period?
★   *e*   How successful was the Evangelical Church? Did it dominate
       the Protestants of Germany?

4   Racial Problems

(a) Hitler on race

History furnishes us with innumerable instances that prove this
law. It shows, with a startling clarity, that whenever Aryans have
mingled their blood with that of an inferior race the result has
been the downfall of the people who were the standard-bearers of
a higher culture. . . .
    In short, the results of miscegenation are always the following:
(a) The level of the superior race becomes lowered;
(b) Physical and mental degeneration sets in, thus leading slowly
but steadily towards a progressive drying up of the vital sap.

> A. Hitler, *Mein Kampf* (London, Hurst and Blackett, 1939),
> p 240

(b) Nazi purity

'The new aristocracy will arise in this way. We shall gather in the
best blood only', said Darré pointing to his iron filing-cabinets.
'Just as we have again produced the old Hanover type of horses
from sires and dams who had little of the old purity left, so we
shall again, in the course of generations breed the type of the
Nordic German by means of recessive crossing. Perhaps we shall
not be able to purify the whole of the German nation again. But

the new German aristocracy will be a pure breed in the literal sense of the term.

20 ... I want all my peasant leaders to enter the S.S.,' Darré said. 'We shall breed the new aristocracy from the human reserves of the S.S. We shall do systematically and on the basis of science and biological knowledge what the old aristocracy of former days did by instinct. In this transitional era we must replace instinct by rational measures. We shall in the first instance make use of the
25 peasantry, insofar as it has the sense to join the movement. We shall also make use of the good heritage of all the old blood aristocracy that has remained pure.'

W. Darré, quoted in H. Rauschning, *Hitler Speaks* (London, Thornton Butterworth, 1939), p 132

(c) *Numbers sterilised*

Congenital feeble-mindedness	203,250
Schizophrenia	73,125
Epilepsy	57,750
Acute Alcoholism	28,500
Manic-depressive insanity	6,000
Hereditary deafness	2,625
Severe hereditary physical deformity	1,875
Hereditary blindness	1,125
St. Vitus' Dance	750
	375,000

W. Devel, *People Under Hitler* (London, Lindsay Drummond, 1942), p 145

(d) *Jewish Stereotypes*

WHY DO WE OPPOSE THE JEWS?
WE are ENEMIES OF THE JEWS, because we are fighters for the freedom of the German people. THE JEW IS THE CAUSE
40 AND THE BENEFICIARY OF OUR MISERY. He has used the social difficulties of the broad masses of our people to deepen the unholy split between Right and Left among our people. He has made two halves of Germany. He is the real cause for our loss of the Great War.
45 The Jew has no interest in the solution of Germany's fateful problems. He CANNOT have any. FOR HE LIVES ON THE FACT THAT THERE HAS BEEN NO SOLUTION. If we would make the German people a unified community and give them freedom before the world, then the Jew can have no place
50 among us. He has the best trumps in his hands when a people

lives in inner and outer slavery. THE JEW IS RESPONSIBLE FOR OUR MISERY AND HE LIVES ON IT.

That is the reason why we, AS NATIONALISTS and AS SOCIALISTS, oppose the Jew. HE HAS CORRUPTED OUR RACE, FOULED OUR MORALS, UNDERMINED OUR CUSTOMS, AND BROKEN OUR POWER.

THE JEW IS THE PLASTIC DEMON OF THE DECLINE OF MANKIND.

> Goebbels pamphlet quoted in L. L. Snyder (ed.), *Documents of German History* (New Brunswick, Rutgers University Press, 1958), p 415

(e) The Crystal Night

November, 25, 1938, Ebenhausen: I am writing under crushing emotions evoked by the vile persecution of the Jews after the murder of vom Rath. Not since the World War have we lost so much credit in the world. But my chief concern is not with the effects abroad, not with what kind of foreign political reaction we may expect – at least not for the moment. I am most deeply troubled about the effect on our national life, which is determined ever more inexorably by a system capable of such things.

Goebbels has seldom won so little credence for any assertion (although there are people among us who swallowed it) as when he said that a spontaneous outburst of anger among the people had caused the outrages and that they were stopped after a few hours. At the same time he laid himself open to the convincing reply that – if such things can happen unhindered – the authority of the state must be in a bad way. As a matter of fact there is no doubt that we are dealing with an officially organized anti-Jewish riot which broke out at the same hour of the night all over Germany! Truly a disgrace! Naive Party functionaries have freely admitted that.

> *The Von Hassell Diaries 1938–44* (London, Hamish Hamilton, 1948), p 20

(f) A defence against anti-semitism

I was never anti-Semitic on the basis of racial principles. At first I thought that the anti-Semitic demands of the Party programme were a matter of propaganda. At that time the Jews, in many respects, held a dominant position in widely different and important fields of German life, and I myself knew many very wise Jews who did not think that it was in the interest of the Jews that they should dominate cultural life, the legal profession, science and commerce to the extent that they did at the time. . . .

The people had a tendency to anti-Semitism at that time.

The Jews had a particularly strong influence on cultural life, and their influence seemed to me particularly dangerous in this sphere because tendencies which I felt to be definitely un-German and
90 inartistic, appeared as a result of Jewish influence, especially in the spheres of painting and music. The Reich Chamber of Culture Law was created, radically excluding the Jews from German cultural life, but with the possibility of making exceptions. I applied these exceptions whenever I was in a position to do so.
95 The law, as I have stated, was decreed by the Reich Cabinet, which bears the responsibility for it.

> Walter Funk interviewed in *Trial of German Major War Criminals*, vol 13 (H.M.S.O., London, 1946), p 70

Questions

a According to extracts *a* and *b* why did the Nazis believe that racial purity was important and how was it to be achieved?

b Why did Darré lay such great stress on the peasantry and the S.S.? What was meant, in extract *b*, by the term the 'new German aristocracy' (line 17)?

★ c What as the purpose of sterilisation and why for these categories in particular (extract *c*)? Why did this policy cease?

★ d According to extract *d*, why were the Jews disliked? How were Jews treated in Germany in the 1930's? Which other groups were badly treated and why?

e What was the 'vile persecution of the Jews after the murder of vom Rath? (extract *e*, lines 60–1)? Why was the writer disgusted with this incident? To what extent was the incident organised by the Nazi party?

★ f How did Funk try to defend himself against the claim of anti-Semitism in extract *f*? What was the general feeling in Germany towards the Jews?

5 Opposition

(a) *A Social Democrat's view*

The number of those who consciously criticize the political objectives of the regime is very small, quite apart from the fact that they cannot give expression to this criticism.

5 . . . They do not want to return to the past and if anyone told them that their complaints about this or that aspect threaten the foundations of the Third Reich they would probably be very astonished and horrified. The mood of 'opposition' consists of an absolute conglomeration of wishes and complaints. The remarks of a low-ranking official of the administration concerning the
10 Jewish question are a good example of this. In response to an

attempt to explain to him the mendacity of the antisemitic propaganda he replied: 'You don't imagine that I am a National Socialist! Not at all. I have many doubts about what is happening. But I must say one thing: It's quite right that nowadays it is no longer the interest of the individual but that of the community that matters. And on the racial question, although I used to reject the loud clamours of the Antisemites and even now do not like Streicher's excesses, after a thorough study of the question I have become convinced that it would be good for Germany to get rid of the Jews.' And yet the man was quite prepared to recognise how dangerous Hitler's policy was in many areas, e.g. rearmament. Conversations with workers and with members of Church circles demonstrate how varied are the causes of the anti-National Socialist mood. Some were and still are very much up in arms about the development of National Socialist Church policy and look at everything in terms of that. However, in conversations with workers the reply to the question of what they thought about the Church dispute was almost invariably: 'That doesn't interest us'. And if one probed deeper there was hardly a trace of any feeling for the inner connection between the struggle of the workers and the other internal tensions of the regime. 'It suits us fine if the Nazis make short work of the Church. Both denominations have deserved it.'

> SPD party report, quoted in J. Noakes and E. Pridham, *Nazism 1919–1945*, a documentary reader, vol 2, (Exeter, University of Exeter, 1983) p 580

(b) Knowledge of the camps?

The German people were well-acquainted with what was happening in concentration camps, and it was well known that the fate of anyone too actively opposed to any part of the Nazi programme was liable to be one of great suffering. Indeed, before the Hitler regime was many months old, almost every family in Germany had received first-hand accounts of the brutalities inflicted in the concentration camps from someone, either in the family circle or in the circle of friends who had served a sentence, and consequently the fear of such camps was a very effective brake on any possible opposition.

> Raymond Geist, quoted in *Trial of German Major War Criminals*, vol 2 (H.M.S.O., London, 1946), p 194

(c) An army plan

Q. We now come to September of 1938 and the crisis which led to the Munich Conference. What were the activities of your group of conspirators at that time?

A. As the crisis gradually came to a head, we tried to convince Halder that he should undertake the putsch at once. Since Halder was quite sure of the situation, Witzleben prepared everything in detail. I shall now describe only the last two dramatic days. On 27 September it was clear that Hitler wanted to go to the last extremity. In order to make the German people war-minded he ordered a parade of the armies in Berlin, and Witzleben had to carry that order out. The parade had entirely the opposite effect. The population, which assumed that these troops were going to war, showed their open displeasure. The troops, instead of jubilation, saw clenched fists, and Hitler, who was watching the parade from the window of the Reich Chancellery, had an attack of anger. He stepped back from his window and said, "With such a people I cannot wage war." Witzleben on his return from the parade, said that he would have liked to have unlimbered the guns outside the Reich Chancellery. On the next morning . . . .

The following morning – this was the 28th – we believed that the opportunity had come to start the revolt. On that morning we too discovered that Hitler had rejected the final offer from the British Prime Minister Chamberlain and had sent the intermediary, Wilson, back with a negative answer. Witzleben received that letter and took it to Halder. He believed that now the proof for Hitler's desire for war had been established, and Halder agreed. Halder visited von Brauchitsch while Witzleben waited in Halder's room. After a few moments Halder came back and said that Brauchitsch now also had realised that the moment for action had arrived and that he merely wanted to go over to the Reich Chancellery to make quite sure that Witzleben and Halder's story was correct. Brauchitsch accordingly went to the Reich Chancellery after Witzleben had told him over the telephone that everything was prepared, and it was at midday on 28 September, when suddenly and contrary to our expectation Mussolini intervened and Hitler, impressed by Mussolini's step, agreed to go to Munich. So at the eleventh hour, the putsch was made impossible.

Dr Gisevius, quoted in *Trial of German Major War Criminals*, vol 12 (H.M.S.O., London, 1946), p 242

Questions

a   What opposition to Hitler did the writer of extract *a* find? Why was it so limited and divided?

b   What opinion was being expressed in extract *b*? How accurate is it? (Compare it to extract *b*, p 92.)

★   c   What aspects of Nazism were attractive to the German people? Did they merely tolerate or actively support the Nazi government?

d Why, according to extract *c*, was a putsch planned and why did it fail? Whose fault was this, indirectly?

★ *e* Why was the army involved in plots against Hitler? Which other groups plotted against Hitler and why were they unsuccessful?

VII   Foreign Policy: Opening Moves, 1933–37

Introduction

Hitler's foreign policy has provoked some of the most bitter disputes amongst historians. At one extreme he is seen as having traditional views of a Greater Germany, a politician who was merely more successful than those of Weimar. Some claim he had no aims at all, merely reacting to events and making up his policies as he went along. At the opposite extreme are those historians who, through the use of selected documents, claim to have discovered blueprints for aggression, longterm plans for the takeover of Europe and eventually the world. As with so many areas of Hitler's policy, he can be seen as either very clever, or very lucky, or a complete megalomanic.

If one tries to pin down Hitler's aims to specific areas, one can still run into trouble. He claimed to want to revise the treaty of Versailles; yet he was content to leave Germany's new western frontiers with France and Belgium intact. He wanted a Greater Germany with all Germans living together; yet he abandoned the South Tyrol to Italy. He may not have been serious about the return of Germany's colonies at all.

Perhaps this is unfair. Some specific aims do crop up often within Hitler's speeches and writings so perhaps the problem lies more in a confusion between aims and methods. The oft-quoted Hossbach Memorandum marks down Austria and Czechoslovakia as targets but says little as regards methods. Many commentators have laid stress on Hitler's ability to use the situation as it arose so one may differentiate between policies initiated by Hitler and those, possibly, in which he took advantage of others' mistakes. If in his early years his policies may seem a little tentative, concentrating on internal affairs such as rearmament, regaining the Saar, remilitarising the Rhineland and his major external idea of a total disaster (the murder of Dolfuss) then one must remember that changes also depend on what other countries are doing. After all, Germany might have remained isolated if Britain and France's response to Italy's invasion of Abyssinia had not alienated Mussolini and pushed him into the arms of Hitler.

1 General Aims

(a) Weimar foreign policy

In my opinion there are three great tasks that confront German foreign policy in the more immediate future.

In the first place the solution of the Reparations question in a sense tolerable for Germany, and the assurance of peace, which is
5 an essential prerequisite for the recovery of our strength.

Secondly, the protection of Germans abroad, those ten to twelve millions of our kindred who now live under a foreign yoke in foreign lands.

The third great task is the readjustment of our Eastern frontiers;
10 the recovery of Danzig, the Polish corridor, and a correction of the frontier in Upper Silesia.

In the background stands the union with German Austria, although I am quite clear that this not merely brings no advantages to Germany but seriously complicates the problem of the German
15 Reich.

If we want to secure these aims, we must concentrate on these tasks. Hence the Security Pact, which guarantees us peace, and makes England, as well as Italy, if Mussolini consents to collaborate, a guarantor of our Western frontiers. The pact also
20 rules out the possibility of any military conflict with France for the recovery of Alsace-Lorraine this is a renunciation on the part of Germany, but, so far, it possesses only a theoretical character, as there is no possibility of a war against France. . . .

The question of a choice between East and West does not arise
25 as the result of our joining the League. Such a choice can only be made when backed by military force. That, alas, we do not possess . . . .

> Stresemann to the former Crown Prince, 7 September 1925, quoted in W. Coole and M. Potter (eds), *Thus Spake Germany* (London, Routledge, 1941), p 339

(b) Hitler's aims

After all, who can deny that the Führer's ideas were perfectly reasonable? Adolf Hitler wanted a strong Reich, at home united
30 through National Socialism against Bolshevism, and armed against all eventualities should a military power arise in the East. Hitler spoke to me repeatedly about the danger of the communist ideology. . . .

A strong Germany was to be the bulwark against this threat to
35 Central Europe. Hitler wanted to revise the impossible frontiers fixed at Versailles, and to alter the position of Danzig and the Polish Corridor, so as to restore agricultural areas to Germany and

to improve her food situation. He wanted to find a solution for
Austria and the Sudetenland. He wanted to be able to sell German
40   products in the Balkans, and to import grain from there. Hitler
wanted friendship with Italy; he was ready to guarantee the
integrity of the Western countries; and he was anxious, in
particular, to come to an agreement with France by waiving his
claims to Alsace-Lorraine. An alliance with Britain was to prevent
45   rivalry at sea and in the air, and although he hoped that he would
be given back one or two colonies, so as to improve the raw
material situation, he did not regard this as a decisive factor, given
reasonable trade agreements. There is no doubt that the Führer
could have settled the ratio of land and sea forces with Britain in
50   the same way as a naval settlement had been reached. As regards
territorial revisions and a gradual solution of the Austrian and
Sudetenland questions, he would have accepted a really long-term
programme. Such in broad outline were Hitler's ideas on Foreign
Policy.

> J. von Ribbentrop, *The Ribbentrop Memoirs* (London,
> Weidenfeld and Nicolson, 1954), p 45

(c) Hitler's methods?

55   Hitler is an Austrian, and the best-known trait of the Austrians is
what is known as their "Schlamperei" – a sort of happy-go-lucky
and haphazard way of doing things. I always felt that Hitler had
his full share of this characteristic. He had all sorts of general plans
in his head, but I greatly doubt if he had preconceived ideas as to
60   how they were to be executed. Unfortunately, as he went on he
became more and more intoxicated with success and confident in
his own greatness and infallibility. His plans grew more grandiose,
and he combined his "Schlamperei" with an amazing mastery of
opportunism. . . . Hitler himself just waited till his opponents
65   made a tactical mistake, and then used the plan which seemed best
to suit both his own general objective and the opportunity afforded
by that mistake.

> N. Henderson, *Failure of a Mission* (London, Hodder and
> Stoughton, 1940), p 185

Questions

a   Explain the terms in extract *a*: (i) 'Reparations question'
(line 3); (ii) the Security Pact (line 17); (iii) the League (line 25).

★ b   What were Stresemann's aims? Were they purely directed at
scrapping the Treaty of Versailles? Why did he oppose a union
with Austria and support the Security Pact?

c   What did Stresemann mean by 'The question of a choice
between East and West does not arise as the result of our
joining the League' (lines 24–5)?

d What were Hitler's aims according to extract *b*? Compare them with extract *a*: in what ways do they agree?

e This extract was written while Ribbentrop, the Nazi foreign minister, was awaiting trial at Nuremberg. In what ways does it try to show that Hitler's demands were reasonable? Why did Ribbentrop feel that Britain and France might not object to them too strongly?

f According to extract *c* what was Henderson's view of Hitler's methods? Is it possible to reconcile the aims of extract *b* with the methods described in this extract?

★ *g* Why have historians argued so much over Hitler's aims and methods? Was he a meticulous planner or a spur-of-the-moment adventurer?

2 Specific Aims

(a) The Treaty of Versailles

Germany is bound hand and foot by Peace Treaties. The whole of German legislation today is nothing else than the attempt to anchor the Peace Treaties in the German people. The National Socialists do not regard these treaties as a law, but as something
5 imposed upon Germany by constraint. We do not admit that future generations who are completely innocent should be burdened by them. If we protest against them with every means in our power then we find ourselves on the path of revolution.

Adolf Hitler at the Leipzig Trial, September 1930, from N. Baynes (trans. and ed.), *The Speeches of Adolf Hitler (1922–1939)*, vol 2 (London, Oxford University Press, 1942), pp 992–3

(b) Greater Germany

Our own task, as we see and understand it, lies in the maintenance,
10 the care, and the betterment of our people; but, strongly as we feel this, we are in like a degree filled with respect for the same outlook amongst folk of other nations. As National Socialists, we reject any desire to turn foreign peoples into Germans; at the same time we oppose with fanaticism any attempt to tear the German
15 from his people. . . . National Socialism knows no policy of correcting frontiers at the expense of foreign peoples. We want no war waged only with the object of bringing over perhaps some millions of folk to Germany who have no wish whatever to be Germans and who cannot be Germans. We shall never attempt to
20 subject folk who in their hearts only hate us as the price of sacrificing on the field of battle millions of those who are dear to us and whom we love. But for this very reason we cling only the

more closely to those who belong to our people, who are of our blood and who speak our language.

Adolf Hitler, 27 May 1933, radio broadcast to Danzig, from N. Baynes (trans. and ed.), *The Speeches of Adolf Hitler (1922–1939)*, vol 2 (London, Oxford University Press, 1942), pp 1061–2

(c) Lebensraum

25　Our economic position is difficult – not, however, because National Socialism rules in Germany, but because in this country there are 140 human beings to the square kilometre, because we have not been given these great natural resources which other nations possess, because, above all, we have a lack of fertile soil. If
30　Great Britain were suddenly to be dissolved to-day and England were to be restricted to its own living space, then perhaps the English would better understand the difficulty of the economic problems which confront us. The fact that Germany has mastered these problems and the manner in which she has done so are
35　miracles and something of which we can really be proud. . . . Germany is a country which has to support 140 people to the square kilometre and possesses no colonial complement whatever; Germany is lacking in numerous raw materials and is neither able nor willing to lead a fraudulent existence on credits; but this same
40　country has reduced its unemployment to zero, and has not merely maintained its standard of life, but has even improved it and has done all this by its own efforts.

Adolf Hitler, speech to Reichstag, 20 February 1938, from N. Baynes (trans. and ed.), *The Speeches of Adolf Hitler (1922–1939)*, vol 2 (London, Oxford University Press, 1942), p 1389

(d) Russia

We National Socialists have purposely drawn a line through the line of conduct followed by pre-War Germany in foreign policy.
45　We put an end to the perpetual Germanic march towards the South and West of Europe and turn our eyes towards the lands of the East. We finally put a stop to the colonial and trade policy of pre-War times and pass over to the territorial policy of the future.

But when we speak of new territory in Europe to-day we must
50　principally think of Russia and the border States subject to her.

Destiny itself seems to wish to point out the way for us here. In delivering Russia over to Bolshevism, Fate robbed the Russian people of that intellectual class which had once created the Russian State and were the guarantee of its existence. For the Russian State
55　was not organized by the constructive political talent of the Slav

element in Russian but was much more a marvellous exemplification of the capacity for State-building possessed by the Germanic element in a race of inferior worth. . . .

For centuries Russia owed the source of its livelihood as a State to the Germanic nucleus of its governing classes. But this nucleus is now almost wholly broken up and abolished. The Jew has taken its place.

This colossal Empire in the East is ripe for dissolution. And the end of the Jewish domination in Russia will also be the end of Russia as a State. We are chosen by Destiny to be the witnesses of a catastrophe which will afford the strongest confirmation of the nationalist theory of race.

A. Hitler, *Mein Kampf* (London, Hurst and Blackett, 1939), p 533

(e) Colonies

As for the claim for the return of the German colonies, it was quite obvious that it was merely being exploited momentarily for propaganda purposes: partly to keep the claim alive for use later, when Germany's aspirations in Europe – a prior consideration – had been achieved and digested; partly to make the German people believe that it was the want of colonies, and not excessive rearmament, which was causing the lack of butter and other comforts. . . . When I spoke to Hitler about colonies in March 1938, his attitude was that the time had not come for discussion about them. They might wait, he said, four, six, or ten years.

N. Henderson, *Failure of a Mission* (London, Hodder and Stoughton, 1940), p 64

Questions

a   Why did Hitler feel Germany did not have to obey the peace treaties according to extract *a*? Which aspects of the treaties did he object to and why?

b   What claims was Hitler putting forward in extract *b*? Which areas of Europe would this have affected?

c   Why did Hitler demand more living space in extract *c*?

★ d   Why did Hitler want to expand into Russia according to extract *d*? Was this for Nazi race motives or for reasons of traditional German foreign policy?

e   According to Henderson in extract *e*, why was Hitler not serious about his claim for colonies? Why did Hitler put forward these claims?

★ f   How good a summary of Hitler's aims in foreign policy are extracts *a–e*?

3 Opening Moves

(a) Leaving the League of Nations

'I had to do it. A liberating deed was necessary – one that should be universally comprehensible. I had to tear the German people out of this clinging network of dependence, vain talk and false conceptions in order to restore our liberty of action. I am not
5 merely an opportunist. Perhaps the difficulties have for the moment been increased. But that is counterbalanced by the increased confidence this deed has won me among the German people. They would not have approved of our going on like a debating society, doing what the Weimar parties had been doing for ten
10 years. As yet, we have not the means of revising the frontiers, but the people believe we have. The people want to see something done; they want no more cheating and swindling. . . . This is the only sort of action, be it wise or not, that the people understand – not this eternal, sterile arguing and haggling, which never leads to
15 any result. The people are tired of being led by the nose.'
> H. Rauschning, *Hitler Speaks* (London, Thornton Butterworth, 1939), p 120

(b) The reintroduction of conscription

"For at this hour the German Government renews before the German people and before the entire world the affirmation of its resolve never to go beyond that which the protection of German honour and the freedom of the Reich demand and especially it
20 affirms that it wished in the nation German armament to create no instrument of military aggression, but on the contrary to create exclusively an instrument for the maintenance of peace.

"The Government of the German Reich further expresses the confident hope that the German people which thus once more
25 finds its way back to its honour may be able in independence and the enjoyment of equal rights to make its contribution to the pacification of the world in free and frank co-operation with the other nations and their Governments.

"It is with this end in view that the Government of the German
30 Reich has to-day decided on the following law."
> Hitler proclamation of 16 March 1935 from N. Baynes (trans. and ed.), *The Speeches of Adolf Hitler (1922–1939)*, vol 2 (London, Oxford University Press, 1942), pp 1210–1211

(c) The assassination of Dollfuss

July 26th – On Monday July 23, after repeated bombings in Austria by Nazis, a boat loaded with explosives was seized on

Lake Constance by the Swiss police. It was a shipment of German bombs and shells to Austria from some arms plant.

35   Today evidence came to my desk that last night, as late as eleven o'clock, the government issued formal statements to the newspapers rejoicing at the fall of Dollfuss and proclaiming the Greater Germany that must follow. The German Minister in Vienna had actually helped to form the new Cabinet. He had, as
40 we now know, exacted a promise that the gang of Austrian Nazi murderers should be allowed to go into Germany undisturbed. But it was realized about 12 o'clock that, although Dollfuss was dead, the loyal Austrians had surrounded the government palace and prevented the organization of a new Nazi regime. They held
45 the murderers prisoners. The German Propaganda Ministry therefore forbade publication of the news sent out an hour before and tried to collect all the releases that had been distributed. A copy was brought to me today by a friend. All the German papers this morning lamented the cruel murder and declared that it was
50 simply an attack of discontented Austrians, not Nazis. News from Bavaria shows that thousands of Austrian Nazis living for a year in Bavaria on German support had been active for ten days before, some getting across the border contrary to law, all drilling and making ready to return to Austria. . . . But now that the drive has
55 failed and the assassins are in prison in Vienna, the German Government denounces all who say there was any support from Berlin.

    I think it will be clear one day that millions of dollars and many arms have been pouring into Austria since the spring of 1933.

      W. E. Dodd Jr and M. Dodd (eds), *Ambassador Dodd's Diary 1933–38* (London, Gollancz, 1941), p 144

(d) The Saar plebiscite

60 "The result of the vote fills me and every one of my colleagues with boundless pride in the German people. It is also a condemnation after the event of the Treaty of Versailles – a condemnation of truly historical magnitude. For in this Treaty this territory was torn from Germany on the basis of the assertion
65 that in it were living 150,000 French people. After fifteen years of government by the League of Nations, that is in the last resort government by France, it is now established that there are but 2,000 French people settled in this territory, this is to say that for every thousand inhabitants of the Saar there are not even as many
70 as four who are French. Can one wonder that a treaty built up on arguments so false as this failed to bring any happiness or blessing to mankind?"

      Adolf Hitler, 16 January 1935, quoted in N. Baynes (trans. and ed.), *The Speeches of Adolf Hitler (1922–1939)*, vol 2 (London, Oxford University Press, 1942) p 1196

(e) Remilitarising the Rhineland

March 7, Saturday. When I reached my office at 9.30 Counsellor
Mayer reported that he must go at once to the Foreign Office to
75   receive information which Dr. Dieckhoff had been asked to give
us. Already the news had come that Hitler was to address the
Reichstag assembly today at 12 o'clock! When Mayer returned at
11 o'clock, he brought a summary of Hitler's propositions: he was
sending some 30,000 troops into the demilitarized zone of the
80   Rhineland; he proposed an agreement with France and Belgium to
demilitarize both sides of the Rhine, also the Dutch border on the
German side; he would denounce the Locarno pact between
Germany, France, Italy and England because France was signing a
pact with Russia, he would return to the League of Nations and be
85   ready to limit aircraft with Western powers, and would demand
the restoration of German colonies.

      W. E. Dodd Jr and M. Dodd (eds), *Ambassador Odd's Diary
      1933–38* (London, Gollancz, 1941), p 144

(f) Italy and Japan

". . . three facts which marked the close of a chapter in German
history:
    '(1) The Treaty of Versailles is dead.'
90   '(2) Germany is free.'
    '(3) The guarantee of our freedom is our own army.'
    . . . "A 'Diktat' that was designed for the eternities we have
destroyed in less than five years and within four years we have
built up again a new army. Added to this, Germany to-day is not
95   isolated but united in close friendship with powerful States. The
natural community of interest between National Socialist Germany
and Fascist Italy has in recent months proved itself more and more
to be an element calculated to safeguard a Europe which is faced
with chaotic madness. It will no longer be possible for anyone
100 simply to ignore this community of will."
    "The same purpose is served by our agreement with Japan – the
purpose to stand together in resistance to an attack on the civilized
world which may take place to-day in Spain, to-morrow in the
East, the day after perhaps somewhere else. In all of us there lives
105 the fervent hope that other Powers, too, may understand the signs
of the times and strengthen this Front which is inspired by reason
and determined to defend peace and our civilization!"

      Adolf Hitler, 7 September 1937, quoted in N. Baynes (trans.
      and ed.), *The Speeches of Adolf Hitler (1929–1939)*, vol 2
      (London, Oxford University Press, 1942), p 1357

Questions

a Why did Hitler leave the League of Nations according to extract *a*? What was his opinion of foreign policy under the Weimar Republic?

b What defence does Hitler give for the reintroduction of conscription in Germany in extract *b*? Why was it announced so publicly?

★ c What evidence does Dodd give in extract *c* to suggest a link between Germany and the assassination of Dollfuss? What other evidence is there?

★ d Why did the assassination of Dollfuss not lead to a German takeover of Austria? How did this incident affect relations between Germany and other countries, Italy in particular?

★ e Why was there a plebiscite in the Saar region according to extract *d*? How did Hitler take advantage of the victory?

★ f Based on the information given in extract *e* and any other available sources show why there was so little opposition from Britain and France to Hitler's remilitarisation of the Rhineland.

g In extract *f* what was the 'Diktat' (line 92)?

h To what extent was there a 'natural community of interest' (line 96) between Germany and Italy, and Germany and Japan at this time?

★ i Comment on the assertions made in this extract from 1937:
  (i) The Treaty of Versailles is dead (line 89).
  (ii) Germany is free (line 90).

4 Plans and Personnel

(a) Hitler's relations with the German Foreign Office

The first time I interpreted for Hitler was on March 25, 1935, ...

Also present were von Neurath, German Foreign Minister, and
5 Ribbentrop, at that time Special Commissioner for Disarmament Questions.

I was surprised when I received the order to attend. It was true that I was senior interpreter at the German Foreign Office, and had worked for practically every German Chancellor and Foreign
10 Minister in the ten years up to the advent of the Hitler Government in January 1933. But the things had changed, Germany had dropped out of the small, man-to-man international discussions, and had adopted the method of notes, memoranda and public pronouncements.
15 Furthermore, Hitler disliked the German Foreign Office and everyone connected with it. In the previous conversations between

him and foreigners the interpreting had been done by Ribbentrop, Baldur von Schirach or some other National Socialist. Our Foreign Office officials were horrified when they heard that Hitler would not even allow State Secretary von Bulow to be present at these highly important discussions with Simon and Eden. In an attempt to ensure that at least one member of the Foreign Office should attend, in addition to von Neurath, they decided to put me forward as interpreter. On being told that I had done good work at Geneva for a long time, Hitler remarked: "If he was at Geneva he's bound to be no good – but so far as I'm concerned we can give him a trial."

> P. Schmidt, *Hitler's interpreter* (London, Heinemann, 1951), p 13

(b) The Hossbach Memorandum

"Berlin, 10th November, 1937. Notes on the conference in the Reichrkanzlei on 5th November, 1937, from 16.15 to 20.30 hours.

Present: The Führer and Reich Chancellor; The Reich Minister for War, Generalfeldmarschall v. Blomberg; The C-in-C. Army, Generaloberst Freiherr von Fritsch; The C-in-C. Navy, Generaladmiral Dr. H. C. Raeder; The C-in-C. Luftwaffe, Generaloberst Goering; The Reich Minister for Foreign Affairs Freiherr v. Neurath; Oberst Hoszach (the adjutant who took the minutes)."

. . . The Führer, had decided not to discuss this matter in the larger circle of the Reich Cabinet, because of its importance. . . .

The Führer then went on: "The aim of German policy is the security and the preservation of the nation and its propagation. This is consequently a problem of space. The German nation comprises eighty-five million people, which, because of the number of individuals and the compactness of habitation, form a homogenous European racial body, the like of which cannot be found in any other country. On the other hand it justifies the demand for larger living space more than for any other nation. If there have been no political measures to meet the demands of this racial body for living space, then that is the result of historical development spread over centuries, and should this political condition continue to exist, it will represent the greatest danger to the preservation of the German nation at its present high level. An arrest of the deterioration of the German element in Austria and in Czechoslovakia is just as little possible as the preservation of the present state in Germany itself.

"Instead of growth, sterility will be introduced, and as a consequence tensions of a social nature will appear after a number of years, because political and philosophical ideas are of a permanent nature only as long as they are able to produce the

basis for the realisation of the actual claim of the existence of a
nation. The German future is therefore dependent exclusively on
the solution of the need for living space. Such a solution can be
sought naturally only for a limited period of about one to three
generations. . . .

"Case 1. Period 1943–45: After this we can only expect a change
for the worse. The rearming of the Army, the Navy and the Air
Force, as well as the formation of the Officers' Corps, are
practically concluded. . . .

"Our material equipment and armaments are modern; with
further delay the danger of their becoming out-of-date will
increase. In particular the secrecy of 'special weapons' cannot
always be safeguarded. Enlistment of reserves would be limited to
the current recruiting age groups and an addition from older
untrained groups would be no longer available.

"In comparison with the rearmament, which will have been
carried out at that time by other nations, we shall decrease in relative
power. Should we not act until 1943–45, then, dependent on the
absence of reserves, any year could bring about the food crisis, for
the countering of which we do not possess the necessary foreign
currency. This must be considered as a 'point of weakness in the
regime.' Over and above that, the world will anticipate our action
and will increase countermeasures yearly. Whilst other nations
isolate themselves we should be forced on the offensive. . . .

"If the Führer is still living, then it will be his irrevocable
decision to solve the German space problem no later than 1943–
45. The necessity for action before 1943–45 will come under
consideration in Cases 2 and 3.

"Case 2. Should the social tensions in France lead to an internal
political crisis of such dimensions that it absorbs the French Army
and thus renders it incapable for employment in war against
Germany, then the time for action against Czechoslovakia has
come.

"Case 3. It would be equally possible to act against Czechoslovakia
if France should be tied up by a war against another State that it
cannot 'proceed' against Germany.

"For the improvement of our military political position it must
be our first aim, in every case of entanglement by war, to conquer
Czechoslovakia and Austria simultaneously, in order to remove
any threat from the flanks in case of a possible advance westwards.
In the case of a conflict with France it would hardly be necessary
to assume that Czechoslovakia would declare war on the same day
as France. However, Czechoslovakia's desire to participate in the
war will increase proportionally to the degree to which we are
weakened. Its actual participation could make itself felt by an
attack on Silesia, either towards the North or the West.

"Once Czechoslovakia is conquered – and a mutual frontier,

Germany-Hungary, is obtained – then a neutral attitude by Poland in a German-French conflict could more easily be relied upon. Our agreements with Poland remain valid as long as Germany's strength remains unshakeable; should Germany have any setbacks then an attack by Poland against East Prussia, perhaps also against Pomerania, and Silesia, must be taken into account."

> *Trial of German Major War Criminals* (H.M.S.O., London, 1946), pp 156–7, 160–1

(c) Armed forces reservations

Fieldmarschal von Blomberg and Generaloberst von Fritsch, in giving their estimate on the situation, repeatedly pointed out that England and France must not appear as our enemies, and they stated that the war with Italy would not bind the French Army to such an extent that it would not be in a position to commence operations on our Western froniter with superior forces. Generaloberst von Fritsch estimated the French forces which would presumably be employed on the Alpine frontier against Italy to be in the region of twenty divisions, so that a strong French superiority would still remain on our Western frontier. The French would, according to German reasoning, attempt to advance into the Rhineland. We should consider the lead which France has got in mobilization, and, quite apart from the very small value of our then existing fortifications – which was pointed out particularly by General Fieldmarschal von Blomberg – the four motorised divisions which had been laid down for the West would be more or less incapable of movement. With regard to our offensive in a south-easterly direction, Fieldmarschal von Blomberg drew special attention to the strength of the Czechoslovakian fortifications, the building of which had assumed the character of a Maginot Line and which would present extreme difficulties to our attack.

. . . In reply to statements by General Fieldmarschal von Blomberg and Generaloberst von Fritsch regarding England and France's attitude, the Führer repeated his previous statements and said that he was convinced of Britain's non-participation and that consequently he did not believe in military action by France against Germany.

> Hossbach memorandum quoted in *Trial of German Major Criminals* (H.M.S.O., London, 1946), pp 162–3

(d) Personnel changes

Not only was Blomberg one of his most trusted advisers, but also one of his most intimate, and possibly most beloved, friends. And this best friend had deceived him. On discovering the truth, Hitler's

first step was to endeavour to persuade the Marshal to allow the marriage to be dissolved, on the ground that he had been inveigled
45 into it under false pretences. Blomberg's refusal to agree to this course shook Hitler's faith in the loyalty of his followers both to himself and to Germany. But worse was to follow. Blomberg had probably never, as a political Marshal and as too subservient to the Nazi civilians, been very popular with the army chiefs. Incidentally
50 he was equally unpopular with the Nazi extremists, as not being one of themselves and as being opposed to their excessive interference in military matters.

Without waiting for Hitler to find his own way out of the impasse, the Commander-in-Chief, General von Fritsch, . . .
55 notified the Führer that army discipline could not tolerate the retention of Blomberg, married to a lady with such a past, in his post as Minister for War. If there is one thing which a dictator dislikes, it is being dictated to. . . .

Hitler himself took over command of the German armed forces
60 and became supreme War Lord, with General Keitel, a serving soldier and a gentleman, performing most of Blomberg's executive functions, but under the direct nominal supervision of the Fuhrer. General von Brauschitsch, a very competent and able officer, succeeded Fritsch as Commander-in-Chief. General Goering was
65 promoted to be a Field-Marshal, thereby becoming the only one on the active list in Germany.

Generally speaking, it may be said that Hitler succeeded in manoeuvring himself out of his difficult position with remarkable adroitness. He had taken a welcome opportunity to effect a purge
70 of the monarchist and conservative elements in the army. He had put its leaders in their place and kept the Party in theirs. The Party had hoped for more drastic action against the army, and the army, though it had met with a decided if inconclusive defeat, was possibly relieved that worse had not befallen it. But the seeds were
75 sown of the absorption of the army within the Party structure.

N. Henderson, *Failure of a Mission* (London, Hodder and Stoughton, 1940), pp 108–9

Questions

a   According to extract *a* what was Hitler's attitude towards the German Foreign Office? What was meant by the phrase, 'If he was at Geneva he's bound to be no good' (lines 25–6)?

b   According to Hitler, in extract *b*, why must there be expansion abroad by 1945 at the latest?

★ c   To what extent, as claimed at the Nuremberg trials, was extract *b* a blueprint for war, proving Hitler's longterm aggressive intentions? Or was it merely a warning to those present that rearmament must proceed more rapidly?

★   *d*   What were Hitler's aims as regards Czechoslovakia, Austria and Poland? How does this outline match with what did actually happen to these countries in the years 1938–39?

     e   According to extract *c* what were Blomberg and Fritsch's reservations concerning Hitler's plans and why did they hold such doubts?

★   *f*   According to Henderson in extract *d*, what excuses did Hitler find to dismiss Blomberg and Fritsch? How accurate a summary of Hitler's intentions is Henderson's final paragraph? Why were Blomberg, Fritsch and Neurath all replaced at this time?

VIII   The Approach to War: Foreign Policy, 1938–39

Introduction

Between 1938–39 the pace of Nazi expansion quickened considerably. In the case of Austria, the Sudetenlands of Czechoslovakia, Memel and Danzig Hitler said he was solely concerned with regaining Germans for Germany. This claim is obviously open to debate. But the idea of revising the seemingly too harsh clauses of the Versailles peace treaty was one that found partial favour with many. Appeasement did suggest a certain readiness in both Britain and France to recognise that Germany had been treated badly in the past and deserved some form of restitution.

It could be argued that Hitler's methods tended to have certain features in common: a demand for an area populated by Germans based on a claim that they were being ill-treated by the government; a rapid rise, reported in Germany, of atrocity stories committed against this minority; vague threats by Hitler that he would intervene. Then the government of the country involved, or its allies, would be panicked into paying Hitler a personal visit and, usually, capitulating to his demands. It is a scenario that fits Austria, the Sudeten crisis and, to a lesser extent, Memel.

Was March 1939 a change in policy? Hitler already had all the Germans from Czechoslovakia, so why should he take over the rest of the country? In some extracts it appears that he was always determined to absorb the entire country at the earliest opportunity. Certainly the crisis precipitated when the Czechs attempted to move against the Slovaks appeared too good a chance for Hitler to miss. But it did show that Hitler wanted more than just all the Germans in Europe and led to a reassessment of policies in Britain and France.

Possibly Britain over-reacted or possibly Hitler had made one move too many. Danzig was German, a point even the British government appears to have been prepared to accept at times in the coming months. But Chamberlain had given a blank cheque of protection to the Poles. They in turn rejected Hitler's demands for Danzig. Hitler expected his non-aggression pact with Russia to discourage Britain from backing Poland but Chamberlain's support remained firm and no Polish delegates went to Berlin. Hitler hesitated for a week and then invaded Poland. World War II had begun. Whether this was a successful or disastrous climax to Hitler's foreign policy is debatable.

1 Austria

(a) Pressure on Austria

Goering's telephone call to his agent:

Goering: '. . . Listen, the main thing is that if Seyss-Inquart takes over all powers of Government he keeps the radio stations occupied.'

5 *Keppler:* 'Well, we represent the government now . . . .'

Goering: 'Yes, that's it. You are the Government. Listen carefully. The following telegram should be sent here by Seyss-Inquart. Take the notes: The provisional Austrian Government, which after the dismissal of the Schuschigg Government, considered it its

10 task to establish peace and order in Austria, sends to the German government the urgent request for support in its task of preventing bloodshed. For this purpose, it asks the German government to send German troops as soon as possible.'

> *Trial of Major German War Criminals*, vol 2 (H.M.S.O., London, 1946), p 420

(b) Chancellor Schuschnigg's last broadcast

'The German Government has handed to the Federal President an

15 ultimatum requiring him to accept a new Chancellor and Government nominated by Germany.

Unless this ultimatum is accepted at once, the German troops will instantly march into Austria. Reports have been circulated that there are disturbances here, that blood is flowing and that the

20 present Government can no longer keep order. I declare before the whole world that these reports are false from A to Z.

The Federal President has charged me to inform the people of Austria that we are giving way to force. To avoid the shedding of German blood, we have ordered our troops to fall back if the

25 Germans should enter Austria.'

> G. Ward Price, *Year of Reckoning* (London, Cassell, 1939), p 97

(c) An interview with Hitler

'These people here are Germans,' retorted Hitler, in indigant tones. 'There is no more sense in a protest from other countries about what I have done than there would be in a note from the

German Government protesting against some development in
30 Britain's relations with Ireland.'
'There is one thing,' I said, 'that the whole world must be
asking itself to-night, and that is – will the turn of Czecho-
Slovakia come next?'
'Was jetzt kommt ist eine Verdauuungs-Pause,' replied the Fuhrer
35 emphatically. 'The next thing is a pause for digestion. If the Czech
Government is wise, it will use the pause to approach me with
some acceptable proposals about the Sudeten question. I am a
realist and I am not unreasonable. Look at the ten-year pact of
non-aggression that I made with Poland. It is based on recognition
40 of the fact that a country of thirty-three million inhabitants must
necessarily have an outlet to the sea. It is hard for us that this
should have to be by means of a corridor running through
German territory, but we realise what it means to the Poles.
There is a German minority in Poland, and a Polish minority in
45 Germany. If the two countries were to quarrel, each would
oppress the minority belonging to the other. It was far better for
Poland and Germany to come to an agreement, and I hope the
example of what has happened in Austria will convince all nations
of the folly of oppressing minorities under alien rule.'
50 Herr Hitler paused a moment.
'You had better not make any reference to Czecho-Slovakia in
what you write,' he said. 'In the first place, it is sure to be
distorted by the Czech Press, and, in the second, it will give the
world the impression that my mind is already occupied with
55 Czecho-Slovakia, which is not the case.
As a matter of fact, even four days ago, I assure you that I had
no idea at all that I would be here today, or that tonight I should
have embodied Austria with the rest of Germany on exactly the
same basis as Bavaria or Saxony.
60 The reason that all this has happened is that Herr Schuschnigg
tried to deceive me, and I will not tolerate being betrayed by
anyone. When I give my word and hand on a matter I stand by it,
and expect anyone who enters into an agreement with me to do
the same. At Berchtesgaden I came to terms with Herr
65 Schuschnigg, under which he was to stop oppressing the Nazi
majority in this country. All he had to do was to carry these terms
out loyally. Instead, he tried to alter the situation to his advantage
by springing this plebiscite upon his country. When I first heard
of his intention, I could not believe it. I sent an emissary by air to
70 Vienna, to find out if the report could possibly be true. This was
Herr Keppler, a financial expert on the Führer's staff.
'As soon as I learned that it was true, I determined to act at once
and the result is that today – the very day that Schuschnigg was
going to hold his plebiscite – I have brought about the union of
75 Austria with Germany. This will be submitted to the national

vote, and you will see the result. It will be a sweeping majority, as there was in the Saar.'

> G. Ward Price, *Year of Reckoning* (London, Cassell, 1939), pp 132–3

Questions

a   In extract *a* who were Schuschnigg (line 9) and Seyss-Inquart (line 2)?

b   According to extract *a* how did the Nazis find an excuse to go into Austria? Why was it important to find such an excuse?

c   How does Schuschnigg's broadcast in extract *b* present a different version of events to that in extract *a*?

d   Why did Hitler want to take over Austria according to extract *c*? How did he defend this occupation?

e   According to extract *c*, what were Hitler's next plans? Do these ideas fit in with the theory that Hitler always planned ahead very carefully?

★ f   Why did Britain and France not oppose the German union with Austria?

2   The Sudetenlands

(a) Hitler's criticisms of Czechoslovakia

'The creation of that country after the war was the utmost folly. It had no scientific basis as a national State, either enthographically, strategically, economically or linguistically. What are the Czechs? They have never had an independent existence except
5   during the Hussite Wars, when they ravaged and burned far into Germany. . . .

For hundreds of years, the Czech territory was a German principality . . . . Everything of value that Bohemia ever developed was derived from German strength.
10   The artificial creation of Czecho-Slovakia would never have come about if Europe had not been divided by the last war. Its continuance depends on the same situation, so that it has always been the ambition of the Czech Government to keep the great European Powers at loggerheads . . . .
15   The Peace Conference pronounced Germany unworthy to rule over negroes in colonies,' exclaimed Herr Hitler bitterly, 'while at the same time it put three and a half million Germans at the mercy of a lot of Czech police-spies. If a powerful Germany had then existed, this would have been impossible, and as soon as Germany
20   became strong again, the Sudetens began to assert themselves. I tell you that the Sudetens despise the Czechs, and that the tyranny of the Czechs over Germans is a thing that cannot and shall not

endure. We publish only a part of what we know about Czech ill-
usage of the Sudetens, for if we made known everything we could
25 not hold our people.'
      G. Ward Price, *Year of Reckoning* (London, Cassell, 1939),
      pp 282–3

(b) Appeasement

On the broadest moral grounds it was thus difficult to justify off-
hand the refusal of the right of self-determination to the 2,750,000
Sudetens living in solid blocks just across Germany's border. Its
flat denial would have been contrary to a principle on which the
30 British Empire itself was founded, and would, consequently,
never have rallied to us the whole-hearted support either of the
British people or of the Empire. There were, on the other hand,
obvious grounds, strategic and economic as well as historic, for
the maintenance of this minority within the Bohemian State, and
35 Dr. Benes, in the months which followed, was quick to take
advantage of these points, and to make them the foundation of his
reluctance to grant an autonomy to the Sudetens which he feared
would merely end in their complete secession.
    But there was a further consideration which carried much
40 weight. If Germany was not always to be allowed to settle
everything in her own way by the display or use of force, then the
Western Powers had got to show courage, and to effect by
diplomatic and peaceful negotiation those revisions of the Versailles
Treaty which might alone be calculated to ensure permanent
45 solutions. The situation afforded the Western Powers an
opportunity to prove that they would not oppose peaceful
evolution, any more than they would condone forcible expansion.
Genuine autonomy for the Sudeten was a moral issue which we
might justifiably press for.
      N. Henderson, *Failure of a Mission* (London, Hodder and
      Stoughton, 1940), p 130

(c) Nazi methods

50 The next four days brought ample proof of how powerful an
instrument broadcasting can be in the hands of a totalitarian
Government. At all hours of the day and night the German
version of conditions in the Sudetenland was dinned into the ears
of the German people. If one could believe the loudspeakers, the
55 Czechs were carrying on a veritable pogrom of the Sudetens.
When the crisis was over, an English colleague of mine who had
been in Czecho-Slovakia at the time, told me that one night when
he was sitting in a beer-house at Eger filled with Sudetens,
someone turned on the wireless. The German news-service was

60   coming through at full blast with details of bloody conflicts
reported to be going on in the streets of that very town. For a
moment, he said, the listeners gazed at each other 'in a wild
surmise' and then burst into a roar of laughter.

    G. Ward Price, *Year of Reckoning* (London, Cassell, 1939),
    pp 248–9

(d) Hitler's decision for action

I) Political requisites: It is my unalterable decision to smash
65   Czechoslovakia by military action in the near future. It is the
job of the political leaders to await or bring about the politically
and militarily suitable moment.

    An inevitable development of conditions inside
Czechoslovakia or other political events in Europe, creating a
70   surprisingly favourable opposition and one which may never
come again, may cause me to take early action.

    Case Green Directive, 30 May 1938, quoted in *Trial of
    German Major War Criminals*, vol 3 (H.M.S.O., London,
    1946), p 43

Questions

a   Why did Hitler claim that the Sudetens were part of Germany
    in extract *a*? Why did he dislike Czechoslovakia?
b   What were Henderson's arguments for and against Hitler's
    claims for the Sudetens in extract *b*?
★ c   What was appeasement? Why did Britain and France adopt this
    policy towards Germany?
d   What was the purpose of extract *c*?
★ e   Why was extract *d* quoted at the Nuremburg War Trials?
★ f   What methods did Hitler use to put pressure on Czechoslovakia
    and on its allies? How successful were these methods?

(e) Chamberlain at Berchtesgaden

By brutally announcing his intention to solve the Czech question
now, even at the risk of a European war, and also by giving the
assurance that Germany would then be satisfied in Europe, he had
moved Chamberlain to agree to support the transfer of the
5   Sudetenland to Germany. Hitler said he had not been able to
refuse a plebiscite. If the Czechs refused, then the way would be
free for the Germans to march in.

    E. von Weizsacker, *Memoirs* (London, Gollancz, 1951),
    p 140

(f) Godesberg

Chamberlain leant back after this exposition with an expression of satisfaction, as if to say: 'Haven't I worked splendidly during these
10 five days?' That was what I felt too, for the agreement of the French, and still more of the Czecho-Slovaks, to a definite cession of territory seemed to me an extraordinary concession. I was the more surprised to hear Hitler say quietly, almost regretfully, but quite definitely: 'I am exceedingly sorry, Mr. Chamberlain, but I
15 can no longer discuss these matters. This solution after the developments of the last few days, is no longer practicable.'

> P. Schmidt, *Hitler's interpreter* (London, Heinemann, 1951),
> p 86

(g) The Godesburg debate

'Have you any idea what the real position is?' I said to them. 'To-day's mysterious proceedings seem to have convinced everyone that war is on the point of breaking out.'
20 'I know,' said Dr. Dietrich, 'but I assure you that the Führer and the Prime Minister are both set on peace, and that to-morrow we shall have to start repairing the damage done by the scare-reports that are circulating to-night.'
'What is going on in there?' I asked. 'For twenty-four hours
25 there has been no news at all, so that it is not surprising that people should be worried.'
'What's going on is that Hitler and Chamberlain are preparing peace, not war, 'replied the German Press Chief emphatically. 'It is a question of procedure, not principle, that divides them.'

> G. Ward Price, *Year of Reckoning* (London, Cassell, 1939),
> p 301

(h) The Munich settlement

30 The final agreement was reached substantially on the lines of the Godesburg memorandum as modified by the final Anglo-French plan. Four areas of progressive occupation by Germany were established with dates. Rights of option were guaranteed, plebiscite areas foreshadowed, and an International Commission nominated
35 to deal with the execution of the final agreement. A possible further Four Power meeting was adumbrated, and the British and French Governments declared their intention to abide by their previous offer of a guarantee of the diminished Czechoslovakia. The German and Italian Governments undertook to participate in
40 this guarantee once the claims of Hungary and Poland had been finally satisfied.

> N. Henderson, *Failure of a Mission* (London, Hodder and
> Stoughton, 1940), p 167

(i) Chamberlain's defence of Munich

Well I have never denied that the terms that I was able to secure at Munich were not those that I myself would have desired. But, as I explained then, I had to deal with no new problem. This was
45 something that had existed ever since the Treaty of Versailles – a problem that ought to have been solved long ago if only the statesmen of the last twenty years had taken broader and more enlightened views of their duty. It had become like a disease which had been long neglected, and a surgical operation was
50 necessary to save the life of the patient. . . .

Really I have no need to defend my visits to Germany last autumn, for what was the alternative? Nothing that we could have done, nothing that France could have done, or Russia could have done could possibly have saved Czecho-Slovakia from invasion
55 and destruction. Even if we had subsequently gone to war to punish Germany for her actions, and if after the frightful losses which would have been inflicted upon all partakers in the war we had been victorious in the end, never could we have reconstructed Czecho-Slovakia as she was framed by the Treaty of Versailles.

Speech at Birmingham, 17 March 1939, quoted in *Documents concerning German–Polish relations* (H.M.S.O., London, 1939), p 6

(j) Churchill's criticism of Munich

60 At Berchtesgaden . . . £1 was demanded at the pistol's point. When it was given, £2 was demanded at the pistol's point. Finally the Dictator consented to take £1 17s 6d and the rest in promises of goodwill for the future. . . . We are in the presence of a disaster of the first magnitude.

Speech of 5 October 1938, quoted in A. Bullock, *Hitler: A Study in Tyranny* (London, Pelican, 1976), p 470

Questions

a   According to extract *e*, why did Chamberlain agree to Hitler's demands? What were his demands?

b   Why was the writer of extract *f* surprised at Hitler's expression?

★ c   Why had the British, French and Czechs agreed to Hitler's demands? Why were they no longer sufficient for Hitler and what new demands did he make?

d   Comment on the line in extract *g*: 'It is a question of procedure, not principle, that divides them' (lines 28–9).

e   According to Henderson in extract *h* what were the final demands of the Munich settlement?

★ f   What was Chamberlain's defence of the Munich settlement in extract *i*? How far did his views support the theory of appeasement? Why was this defence made in public on 17 March 1939?

★   *g*   Was Churchill's accusation in extract *j* a just one?

3   The Slovak Crisis

(a) *The crisis*

The brew was, in fact, already being stirred by his followers. The Vienna radio was busily inciting Slovaks against Czechs, and a fraternal quarrel between those two Slav kinsfolk was being worked up, to serve Hitler with another of those openings which
5   he was so skilful in turning to his own advantage. Within a week the quarrel had become so embittered that on March 10th the Czech President dismissed the Slovak Prime Minister, Father Tiso, occupied Bratislava with Czech troops and gendarmerie, and forcibly installed another Government there with a nominee
10   at its head, Karel Sidor, who enjoyed the confidence of Prague. Once again, Hitler's opponents Slovaks and Czechs alike, had made a false move and played into his hands. The chance was too good a one for Hitler's opportunism to let slide, and, arrogantly regardless of the consequences, he proceeded once more to pull
15   the appropriate plan out of its drawer and to act like lightning.

        N. Henderson, *Failure of a Mission* (London, Hodder and Stoughton, 1940), p 201

(b) *Hacha visits Hitler*

At night Hacha was received at the Reich Chancellery, where Hitler announced his intention to occupy Bohemia and Moravia. I had a long talk with Chwalkowski who in the light of developments accepted our point of view. Before signing the
20   agreement Hacha had telephoned Prague to obtain his government's approval. There was no Czech protest, and Hacha gave the order to give the German troops a friendly welcome. The entry and occupation then passed off without incidents.

        J. von Ribbentrop, *The Ribbentrop Memoirs* (London, Weidenfeld and Nicolson, 1954), pp 94–5

(c) *Another version*

I was not surprised when a few days before March 13th, I learnt
25   that the march into Czech territory had been fixed for the early hours of March 15th.

    Hacha and Chwalkowski too had seen the approach of disaster, and this was their last-minute, desperate effort to save their country. They sought an interview with Hitler, who agreed to receive them in Berlin. They were met at the station with all the honours due to the head of a State. . . .

In Hitler's gloomy office the realities of the situation emerged, by contrast, even more starkly. Here was no intimate discussion between man and man. There were a number of people present but Hacha, Chwalkowski, the rest, even Goering and Ribbentrop were the audience, Hitler the speaker with one long accusation against the Czechs by Hitler, who now repeated the same calendar of crimes which he had already exhaustively enumerated to the British and French. No new point was raised. As compared with the Benes regime, Hitler asserted nothing had changed – under the surface the Benes spirit lived on in the new Czecho-Slovakia. He did not mean, he said, to imply any distrust of Hacha; in Germany they were convinced of his loyalty. But, for the security of the Reich, it was necessary for Germany to assume a protectorate over the remnant of Czecho-Slovakia. . . . Hacha and Chwalkowski sat as though turned to stone while Hitler spoke. Only their eyes showed that they were alive. It must have been an extraordinarily heavy blow to learn from Hitler's mouth that the end of their country had come. They had set out from Prague in the hope that they would be able to treat with Hitler but already . . . they had been told by the Czech minister in Berlin that German troops had crossed their frontier at Ostrau. Then Hacha had had to sit and wait for hours at the Adlon Hotel for a telephone call from the Chancellery. Hitler finally received him at one o'clock in the morning.

It was astonishing how the old gentleman kept his composure with Hitler after all this strain. 'The German troops' entry can't be hindered,' said Hitler. 'If you want to avoid bloodshed you had better telephone to Prague at once, and instruct your Minister of War to order the Czech forces to offer no resistance.' With these words Hitler brought the interview to an end. Hacha and Chwalkowski spoke to Prague, and Goering and I left the room while they continued their conversation in Czech. The connection did not seem very good, for Chwalkowski, who spoke first, had to raise his voice and speak very slowly.

I was now busily preparing a fair copy, only a few lines long, of the communiqué: 'At the meeting (of Hitler and Hacha) the serious situation arising from the events of recent weeks in what was formerly Czecho-Slovak territory was frankly considered. The conviction was expressed on both sides that all endeavours must be directed to securing tranquillity, order and peace in that part of Central Europe. The President of the State of Czecho-Slovakia has declared that, in order to serve his aim and final pacification, he confidently lays the fate of the Czech people and

country in the hands of the Führer of the German Reich. The
Führer has accepted this declaration, and has announced his decision
to take the Czech people under the protection of the German
Reich and to accord it to autonomous development of its national
life in accordance with its special characteristics.'
The text, which had been prepared beforehand by Hitler, was
signed by him and Hacha as well as by Ribbentrop and
Chwalkowski, on March 15th at 3.55 a.m.

> P. Schmidt, *Hitler's interpreter* (London, Heinemann, 1951),
> pp 123–6

(d) Hitler's proclamation, 16 March 1939

For a millenium the territories of Bohemia and Moravia belonged
to the living space (Lebensraum) of the German people. Violence
and stupidity tore them arbitrarily from their ancient historic
setting and at last through their inclusion in the artificial
construction of Czechoslovakia created a hotbed of continual
unrest. Year by year the danger grew ever greater that from this
area as had already happened once in the past, there might arise a
new, vast menace to the peace of Europe. For the Czechoslovak
state and its authorities had not been able to organise on a
reasonable basis the common life of the groups of people arbitrarily
united within it and thus to awaken and maintain the interest of all
concerned in the preservation of the State of which they all were
members. The Czechoslovak State has thus proved its inability to
live its own internal life and in consequence has now in fact fallen
into dissolution.
But the German Reich cannot tolerate permanent disturbances
in these territories which are of such decisive importance, alike for
its own calm and security, as well as for the general welfare and
the general peace.

> N. Baynes (trans. and ed.), *The Speeches of Adolf Hitler
> (1922–1939)*, vol 2 (London, Oxford University Press,
> 1942), p 586

(e) British objections

What conclusions are we to draw from this conquest of
Czechoslovakia? Are we to believe that German policy has thus
entered upon a new phase? Is German policy any longer to be
limited to the consolidation of territory predominantly inhabited
by persons of German race? Or is German policy now to be
directed towards domination over non-German peoples? These are
very grave questions which are being asked in all parts of the
world today. The German action in Czechoslovakia has been
furthered by new methods, and the world has lately seen more

than one new departure in the field of international technique. Wars without declarations of war. Pressure exercised under threat of immediate employment of force. Intervention in the internal struggles of other states. Countries are now faced with the
115 encouragement of separatism, not in the interest of seperatist or minority interests but in the imperial interests of Germany. The alleged ill-treatment of German minorities in foreign countries which, it is true, may sometimes, perhaps often, arise from natural causes, but which may also be the subject and result of provocation
120 from outside, is used as a pretext for intervention.

> Speech by Lord Halifax, 20 March 1939, in *Speeches on Foreign Policy by Viscount Halifax* (London, Oxford University Press, 1940), p 244

Questions

a How, according to Henderson in extract *a*, did the Slovaks and Czechs play into Hitler's hands? What interpretation of Hitler's methods does this extract put forward?

b In extract *b* how does Ribbentrop try to portray these events in a way favourable to the Nazis?

c Extract *c* describes the same events as those in extract *b*. In what ways does it differ from the preceding extract? What does it suggest concerning Hitler's methods?

d Compare the communiqué at the end of extract *c* with Hitler's excuses for going into Austria (extract *c*, pp 118–20) and the Sudetenland (extract *a*, pp 120–21).

e In extract *d* why does Hitler refer to the territories of Bohemia and Moravia rather than to Czechoslovakia? What reasons for occupying these areas does this proclamation give?

★ f What questions did Halifax raise over the takeover of Czechoslovakia in extract *e*? What Nazi methods was he worried about? How did Britain react to this takeover and why?

★ g Did Hitler's takeover of Czechoslovakia fit in with his public proclamations of his aims in foreign affairs? Was the takeover a mistake in relation to its effect on world opinion?

4 Poland and the Danzig Question

(a) Hitler's wishes

In order finally to clear up the questions which were still in suspense between the two countries one must not restrict oneself to the more negative agreement of the year 1934 but must seek to bring the individual problems to a final settlement by mutual
5 agreement. On the German side apart from the question of

Memel, which would find its settlement in the way which the Germans desired (it looked as though the Lithuanians were willing to cooperate in a reasonable solution), so far as the relation between Germany and Poland is concerned there was the very
10 difficult problem for German susceptibilities of the Corridor and Danzig: for that a solution must be found. In his view, in this case solutions were to be sought along quite new paths, and traditional forms must be abandoned.

One could, for example, in the case of Danzig, conceive of a
15 settlement by which this city in accordance with the wish of its population might be restored so far as its political position was concerned to the German community; in any such arrangements Polish interests especially in the sphere of economics, must of course be fully and completely safeguarded. That would
20 undoubtedly be also in Danzig's interest, for Danzig in economics could not live without a hinterland, and thus he, the Führer, could imagine a formula by which Danzig could politically form part of the German community, while in the economic sphere it remained Polish.
25 Danzig is German, will always remain German, and sooner or later will come to Germany.

As concerned the Corridor which for Germany, as he had already said, presented a difficult psychological problem the Führer pointed out that for the Reich the connexion with East Prussia
30 was of vital interest just as was for Poland the connexion with the sea. Perhaps here, too, one could do justice to the interests of both parties through seeking a solution by the use of completely new methods.

Adolf Hitler's speech of 5 January 1939 from N. Baynes (trans. and ed.), *The Speeches of Adolf Hitler (1922–1939)*, vol 2 (London, Oxford University Press, 1942), p 1564

(b) Specific demands

I have had the following proposal submitted to the Polish
35 Government:-
1) Danzig returns as a Free State into the framework of the German Reich.
2) Germany receives a route through the Corridor and a railway line at her own disposal possessing the same extra territorial
40 status for Germany as the Corridor itself has for Poland.
In return, Germany is prepared:-
1) To recognise all Polish economic rights in Danzig.
2) To ensure for Poland a free harbour in Danzig of any size desired which would have completely free access to the sea.
45 3) To accept at the same time the present boundaries between Germany and Poland and to regard them as ultimate.

4) To conclude a twenty-five-year non-aggression treaty with Poland, a treaty therefore which would extend far beyond the duration of my own life.

> Adolf Hitler's speech of 28 April 1939, in *Documents concerning German–Polish relations* (H.M.S.O., London, 1939), p 22

(c) Danzig or Poland?

50 Danzig is not the subject of the dispute at all. It is a question of expanding our living space in the East and of securing our food supplies, of the settlement of the Baltic problem. Food supplies can only be expected from thinly populated areas. Over and above the natural fertility, thorough going, German exploitation will
55 enormously increase the surplus.

> Adolf Hitler's speech in conference of 23 May 1939, quoted in *Trial of Major German War Criminals*, vol 3 (H.M.S.O., London, 1946), p 279

(d) The British position

. . . Apparently the announcement of a German–Soviet Agreement is taken in some quarters in Berlin to indicate that intervention by Great Britain on behalf of Poland is no longer a contingency that need be reckoned with. No greater mistake could be made.
60 Whatever may prove to be the nature of the German–Soviet Agreement, it cannot alter Great Britain's obligation to Poland which His Majesty's Government have stated in public repeatedly and plainly, and which they are determined to fulfil. . . .

If the case should arise, they are resolved, and prepared, to
65 employ without delay all the forces at their command, and it is impossible to foresee the end of hostilities once engaged. It would be a dangerous illusion to think that, if war once starts, it will come to an early end even if a success on any one of the several fronts on which it will be engaged should have been secured.
70 Having thus made our position perfectly clear, I wish to repeat to you my conviction that war between our two peoples would be the greatest calamity that could occur. I am certain that it is desired neither by our people, nor by yours, and I cannot see that there is anything in the questions arising between Germany and
75 Poland which could not and should not be resolved without the use of force, if only a situation of confidence could be restored to enable discussions to be carried on in an atmosphere different from that which prevails today.

> Letter from Chamberlain to Hitler, 22 August 1939, quoted in *Documents concerning German–Polish relations* (H.M.S.O., London, 1939), p 97

Questions

★   a   In extract *a* what was the 'more negative agreement of the year 1934' (line 3)? Why did Germany make this agreement?

★   b   What was the 'question' of Memel (line 5)? How was this problem finally solved?

      c   What demands did Hitler make on Poland in extracts *a* and *b*?

★   d   How does extract *c* compare with Hitler's offer in extract *a*? Why was this document quoted in the Nuremberg War Trials?

★   e   What was the German–Soviet Agreement referred to in extract *d* (lines 60–1)? Why did both sides sign it?

★   f   In what ways did the British try to bring about a peaceful settlement of the Polish dispute?

★   g   Why did Hitler find himself involved in a major war as a result of the invasion of Poland?